VISION TO VICTORY

DEFINE CLEAR GOALS, BUILD HABITS, OVERCOME PROCRASTINATION, AND ACHIEVE DREAMS

DILIP PATIL

Copyright © 2024 by Dilip Patil

All rights reserved.

No part of this workbook may be reproduced, distributed, or transmitted in any form or by any means, including photocopying, recording, or other electronic or mechanical methods, without the prior written permission of the author, except in the case of brief quotations embodied in critical reviews and specific other non-commercial uses permitted by copyright law. For permission requests, please get in touch with the author at patildilip23@gmail.com

Disclaimer

This workbook is for educational and personal development purposes only. The author does not guarantee specific outcomes or results, as individual success depends on personal effort, commitment, and circumstances.

TABLE OF CONTENTS

WHY THIS BOOK .... **V**
GOAL MASTERY SERIES .... **VII**
INTRODUCTION **1**
YOUR FREE COMPANION WOOKBOOK **7**
1   DEFINE YOUR WHY **8**
    1.1   WHY GOALS MATTER "WHY" 10
    1.2   ALIGN GOALS WITH YOUR CORE VALUES 13
    1.3   VISUALIZE YOUR FUTURE SELF 15
2   SET SMART GOALS **18**
    2.1   THE SMART FRAMEWORK 19
    2.2   STRETCH GOALS FOR EXTRA MOTIVATION 23
    2.3   BREAK BIG GOALS INTO SUBGOALS 24
3   CRAFT A VISION **28**
    3.1   WHAT MAKES A GREAT VISION STATEMENT 29
    3.2   STEPS TO CRAFT YOUR VISION 31
    3.3   BRINGING YOUR VISION TO LIFE 34
4   BUILD HABITS **38**
    4.1   THE HABIT LOOP 40
    4.2   THE 2-MINUTE RULE 42
    4.3   TRACK YOUR PROGRESS 44
5   CREATE ROUTINES **48**
    5.1   DESIGN ROUTINES 50
    5.2   GOAL CHECKLISTS 54
    5.3   CREATE FLEXIBILITY 56
6   BEAT PROCRASTINATION **59**
    6.1   PROCRASTINATION TRIGGERS 61
    6.2   TAKE ACTION BEFORE YOUR BRAIN STOPS 63
    6.3   BREAK TASKS INTO CHUNKS 64

7 PLAN AND PRIORITIZE 69

    7.1   TURN BIG GOALS INTO MANAGEABLE STEPS 71
    7.2   PRIORITIZING TASKS THAT MATTER 73
    7.3   STAYING ORGANIZED AND ON TRACK 76

8 STAY ACCOUNTABLE 80

    8.1   ACCOUNTABILITY PARTNERS AND GROUPS 82
    8.2   MAKE YOUR GOALS VISIBLE 85
    8.3   STAY ACCOUNTABLE TO YOURSELF 87

9 CELEBRATE WINS 92

    9.1   THE POWER OF SMALL WINS 94
    9.2   REWARD SYSTEMS FOR MILESTONES 96
    9.3   TRACK SUCCESS AND REFLECTION 99

10 FROM VISION TO VICTORY 104

    10.1   REFLECT ON PROGRESS 106
    10.2   ADJUST FOR FUTURE GOALS 108
    10.3   MAINTAIN LONG-TERM SUCCESS 110

CONCLUSION 115

    SUMMARY 115
    FINAL BOOST 118

YOUR NEXT STEP TO SUCCESS 120

APPENDICES 121

    APPENDIX A: SMART GOAL PLANNER TEMPLATE 121
    APPENDIX B: HABIT TRACKER SHEET 123
    APPENDIX C: DAILY ROUTINE CHECKLIST 124
    APPENDIX D: RECOMMENDED BOOKS AND RESOURCES 126

ACKNOWLEDGMENTS 130

NEXT IN THE GOAL MASTERY SERIES 131

SHARE YOUR EXPERIENCE 133

ABOUT THE AUTHOR 135

OTHER BOOKS BY DILIP PATIL 138

WHY THIS BOOK

What separates those who dream from those who achieve? You are not alone if you have ever set a goal but struggled to follow through. Most people start with enthusiasm but lose steam when life becomes busy, obstacles arise, or motivation fades. The difference between dreamers and doers isn't willpower—it's clarity, intentional action, and consistent effort.

That's where this book comes in.

Vision to Victory is designed to help you define your goals and create the systems and habits needed to achieve them. It bridges the gap between where you are today and where you want to be by providing practical tools that guide you every step. This book is not about lofty ideas or abstract theories. It's a hands-on, actionable guide to building your envisioned life—one step at a time.

Here's why these matters:

- Clarity creates momentum. When you know precisely what you want and why it matters, it becomes easier to take action.
- Consistency beats motivation. Tiny, repeated actions are more powerful than occasional bursts of effort.

- Habits led to results. Goals alone don't lead to success—your daily routines do.

This book is here to help you overcome the common roadblocks that prevent most people from achieving their dreams: procrastination, distractions, and the fear of failure. By the time you finish, you'll know how to set meaningful goals and have built the mindset, habits, and routines needed to make them a reality.

No matter what your goal is—whether it's improving your health, building a business, or pursuing a passion project—this book will help you stay focused and take consistent action until you achieve it. The journey from vision to victory begins now.

GOAL MASTERY SERIES

Vision to Victory is the first book in the Goal Mastery Series, a step-by-step guide to unlocking your potential and achieving lasting success. This series simplifies goal-setting, habit-building, and personal growth into practical, actionable strategies to help you progress in every area of life.

Why a Series?

Achieving goals takes focus, persistence, and adaptability. The Goal Mastery Series equips you with the tools and mindset to overcome challenges and stay consistent.

Vision to Victory lays the foundation—teaching you how to define your vision, set clear goals, build habits, and beat procrastination. Future books will explore time management, momentum, and resilience.

Ready to Begin?

Your journey starts here. Let's take the first step together toward your best life!

Introduction

Imagine sitting across from the version of yourself five years from now. What would they say about your life today? Are you on track to achieve your dreams, or are there goals you keep putting off, waiting for "the right moment"?

We all have a vision of the life we want—building a successful career, creating financial freedom, achieving a fitness goal, or finding time for personal passions. But far too often, life gets in the way. We know what we want, yet we struggle to take action. We get distracted, procrastinate, or feel overwhelmed. Days turn into months; before we know it, another year has passed with dreams still stuck in our minds instead of coming to life.

This book has been written to help you bridge the gap between where you are today and where you want to be. No matter your goal, its principles will equip you with the clarity, habits, routines, and mindset needed to achieve it.

What You Will Gain from This Book

By the time you finish reading Vision to Victory, you will have the tools to:

- Define meaningful goals that align with your deepest values and purpose.

- Build small, powerful habits that compound into remarkable results over time.
- Break free from procrastination by understanding your mental blocks and triggers.
- Create routines and systems that make progress effortless.
- Stay accountable and motivated, even when life throws challenges your way.
- Celebrate your wins and keep building momentum toward your dreams.

Whether your goals are personal or professional, this book will guide you step-by-step toward the finish line.

Why I Wrote This Book

Let me share a bit of my journey with you.

There was a time in my life when I felt stuck. I had big dreams, but those dreams felt distant, almost unreachable. Whenever I tried to start something meaningful—a personal project or a goal at work—I would lose momentum after the initial excitement faded. I had put things off, waiting for "inspiration" or "the perfect moment." But the perfect moment never came.

The turning point came when I realized success is about something other than waiting for motivation. It's about building habits, creating routines, and setting clear goals that keep you on track—even when you don't feel like it. Once I embraced this mindset, everything changed.

This book is a product of what I have learned through personal experience and studying what works for high achievers in various fields. I have condensed the best strategies and tools into a practical guide anyone can follow. There is no fluff, no vague advice—just actionable steps to help you move from vision to victory.

What Makes This Book Different?

You have probably read goal-setting advice before. Maybe you have heard about setting SMART goals or building better habits. However, the problem with many self-help books is that they offer advice without showing you how to implement it consistently in your life. This book is designed to be actionable, practical, and easy to follow.

Every chapter builds on the previous one, guiding you through a transformation process. The book isn't just about setting goals—it's about developing a system of success that becomes a natural part of your life. Every step is detailed, from creating your personal "why" to building small habits, overcoming procrastination, and staying accountable.

The result? Not just short-term success but sustainable progress that leads to long-term victory.

How to Use This Book Effectively

This isn't just a book to read—it's a book to apply. As you move through each chapter, you will find exercises, tools, and actionable strategies designed to help you take tangible steps toward your goals. Here are a few tips to get the most out of this book:

1. **Take Notes and Reflect:** Keep a journal or notebook nearby to jot down key insights and your thoughts as you read. The more you engage with the content, the more it will stick.
2. **Do the Exercises:** Every chapter has practical exercises and worksheets to help you apply your knowledge. Don't skip them! These small actions will build momentum and keep you moving forward.
3. **Start Small:** Some of the ideas in this book may challenge you to step outside your comfort zone. That's okay. Growth happens in small, manageable steps. As you go through the chapters, pick just one action you can take immediately, no matter how small. Action creates momentum.
4. **Revisit Key Sections:** Goal-setting and habit-building are ongoing processes. Whenever you hit a roadblock, return to the relevant chapter and use the strategies to get back on track.

5. **Celebrate Your Progress:** Success isn't just about the big wins. Throughout this journey, it's essential to celebrate every small step forward. Acknowledging your progress keeps you motivated and builds confidence.

What Happens When You Take Action?

You need to know that taking consistent action—no matter how small—will change your life.

You don't need to be perfect, and you don't need to have everything figured out from the start. All you need is a vision of what you want and the willingness to take the next step. This book will show you how to stay focused on your goals, build momentum, and keep moving forward—especially when things get tough.

By the end of Vision to Victory, you won't just know how to set meaningful goals. You'll know how to build the habits, routines, and mindset that will carry you to success.

Your Journey Starts Now

There's no better time than today to begin. Whatever goals you have—launching a new business, improving your health, writing a book, or achieving personal growth—it all starts with taking the first step.

This book is your roadmap. It will help you clarify your vision, define your path, and give you the tools to stay on course until you achieve victory. The journey won't always be easy, but it will be worth it.

So, are you ready to get started? Let's take that first step together. The life you have always envisioned is within reach and begins now.

****

YOUR FREE COMPANION WORKBOOK

Congratulations on starting your journey with Vision to Victory! This book has powerful strategies to help you define your goals, build habits, and achieve your dreams. But reading alone is just the first step. To truly transform your vision into action, you must practice these strategies.

I created the Vision to Victory Personal Workbook—a free, downloadable companion.

This workbook includes practical exercises and prompts aligned with the chapters of this book to help you take measurable steps toward your goals. Download it now: Click the image or scan the QR code with your phone to get your free copy instantly!

1   Define Your Why

"When you know your 'why,' you can endure any 'how. — Friedrich Nietzsche.

Remember when you felt fully committed to something that mattered deeply to you? Maybe it was finishing a challenging course, working tirelessly to achieve a personal milestone, or stepping outside your comfort zone to make a difference for someone you love. What kept you going through the hard days? It wasn't just the goal itself—the reason behind the goal, the deep sense of meaning and purpose that pushed you forward when giving up felt easier.

This sense of purpose—your "why"—separates goals that inspire us from those that feel like chores. When a goal is tied to something significant, it becomes more than a task on a checklist. It becomes a part of who you are and what you stand for. Purpose fuels perseverance, helping you push through distractions, setbacks, and the inevitable moments of doubt that arise along the way. Without a clear "why," even the best intentions can crumble under the weight of life's challenges.

Imagine this: You decide to start a fitness journey. If your goal is vague—like losing a few pounds or "getting healthier"—your motivation might fizzle out after a few weeks. But what if your "why" is deeply personal, like staying healthy to keep up with your children or building strength to recover from an injury? Suddenly, the goal isn't just about the outcome—it's about the life you want to live. That emotional connection to your purpose transforms your goal into something bigger, something worth fighting for.

The truth is that success doesn't just come from having the right strategies or tools. It comes from knowing what drives you—what lights a fire inside you, even when the path is difficult. Your "why" is your anchor, grounding you when distractions pull you off course. It's also your fuel, energizing you to take the next step, no matter how challenging. When you know your "why," you gain clarity, resilience, and focus. You stop going through the motions and start living with intention.

In this chapter, we'll dive into what it means to find your "why" and why it's the foundation of every meaningful goal. You'll uncover the deeper reasons behind your ambitions and learn how aligning your goals with your values can create a powerful sense of purpose. We'll explore the connection between purpose and resilience—how a strong "why" helps you stay committed through setbacks—and introduce practical strategies to craft a "why" that feels authentic, personal, and deeply tied to your vision for your life. By the end of this chapter, you'll clearly understand your "why"—the driving force that makes your goals achievable and sustainable. This "why" will become your guiding star, reminding you why you started, helping you navigate challenges, and keeping you focused on turning your vision into victory.

Let's begin this journey by looking inward. Let's uncover the deeper meaning behind your dreams so that every step forward is grounded in purpose and every action is aligned with the life you truly want to create.

1.1 WHY GOALS MATTER "WHY"

Imagine two people who have decided to run a marathon. One is doing it because they think it would be a good fitness goal and say they have completed a marathon. The other is running to raise money in honor of a loved one who passed away from a heart condition.

Both runners will face the same obstacles—long training sessions, sore muscles, and moments of self-doubt. However, when training becomes burdensome, the person with a meaningful purpose will have an extra source of strength. Their "why" fuels them to keep going, no matter how hard it gets. This power of purpose transforms an ordinary goal into something deeply significant, making every challenge worth facing.

When you have an intense "why," it becomes easier to endure difficulties and stay committed; purpose gives you the resilience to keep moving forward, even when progress feels slow or setbacks appear. A powerful "why" turns your goals from "nice-to-haves" into "must-haves," giving you a sense of urgency and determination.

Exercise

Let's examine the purpose behind your goals. This exercise will help you uncover the more profound reasons driving you so that your goals feel more meaningful and personal.

1. **Choose a Goal:** Think of an essential goal for you now. It could be a career goal, a health goal, or something personal you've wanted to accomplish for a long time. Please write it down in a notebook or journal.
2. **Ask Yourself "Why?"** Once you have your goal, ask yourself, "Why do I want to achieve this goal?" Don't settle for a surface-level answer. Keep digging until you reach the core reason that resonates with you emotionally.
3. **Go Deeper:** After answering, ask "why" again and again for each answer you write down. This technique is often called the "Five Whys," developed by Sakichi Toyoda, the founder of

Toyota Industries in the 1930s. By repeatedly asking "why," you'll move from general reasons to the real, personal motivators behind your goal. For example, your Goal is to start a side business.

- Why? To earn extra income.
- Why? So I can have financial security and freedom.
- Why? Because I want to provide a better future for my family and have time to enjoy life with them.
- Why? Because I want to break free from a stressful work environment and live on my terms.
- Why "I want to create financial freedom and a better future for my family while having the flexibility to live on my terms."

4. **Reflect on Your Final Answer:** After identifying your "why," pause and reflect. Does it resonate with you emotionally? Is it powerful enough to keep you committed, even when challenging? Write down any thoughts or insights that come to mind.

This deeper "why" is what will keep you grounded and motivated. Remember, the stronger your "why," the more robust your commitment to seeing your goals through.

1.2 ALIGN GOALS WITH YOUR CORE VALUES

Now that you have identified your "why," let's discuss aligning your goals with your core values. Values are the guiding principles that give your life meaning and shape your decisions. When your goals align with your values, they feel authentic and fulfilling. But when there's a misalignment, you will feel inner conflict, leading to stress, frustration, and even burnout.

For example, let's say you set a goal to advance in your career by working longer hours. If one of your core values is family, working late every night might create tension and resentment, pulling you away from what's most important to you. In contrast, you will feel more balanced and motivated if you aim to achieve career success while maintaining quality time with your family.

Exercise

This exercise will help you clarify your core values and ensure your goals reflect them.

1. **List Your Values:** Take a few minutes to write down the five to ten values most important to you. If you're not sure where to start, here are some examples:
   - Family
   - Health
   - Creativity

- Personal Growth
- Freedom
- Integrity
- Service to Others
- Financial Security

Reflect on moments when you felt fulfilled and proud—these moments often reveal your values.

2. **Check for Alignment:** Review your goal and see if it aligns with your top values. For each value, ask yourself: "Does this goal honor this value?" If not, consider adjusting your goal to reflect better what truly matters to you.

3. **Refine Your Goal if Needed:** If you notice any misalignment, consider refining your goal or adjusting your approach. For instance, if "health" is a core value, but your goal requires sacrificing sleep, you might look for ways to achieve your goal while maintaining a healthy lifestyle.

Example

If "service" is valuable, you might set a goal to volunteer monthly, mentor others in your field, or start a community project. When your goals reflect your values, you'll find that every step forward feels purposeful and rewarding.

Aligning your goals with your values creates a sense of integrity and fulfillment. Your actions will feel authentic, and you'll experience less resistance on your journey.

1.3 VISUALIZE YOUR FUTURE SELF

With your "why" and values in place, it's time to connect emotionally with the person you're becoming. Visualization is a powerful technique that allows you to experience your future mentally. By visualizing your ideal self, you build confidence, reduce self-doubt, and create a clear image of the life you're working toward.

Imagine the best version of yourself five or ten years from now. What does your life look like? How do you feel? Visualization helps you feel the emotions of success before you reach it, making the journey more exciting and motivating.

Exercise

- **Find a Quiet Space:** Sit somewhere comfortably, close your eyes, and take a few deep breaths to relax. Let go of any distractions and focus your mind.
- **Visualize Your Ideal Life:** Picture yourself living your ideal life five or ten years from now. Visualize details—where you live, your daily

routine, who you spend time with, and what you've achieved.

- **Focus on Emotions:** Imagine the pride, happiness, and fulfillment of achieving your goals. Feel the joy of living a life that aligns with your "why" and values. The stronger your emotional connection to this vision, the more powerful it will be as a motivator.
- **Write It Down:** After visualization, open your eyes and write down what you saw and felt. Describe your future self in as much detail as possible. This will serve as a written reminder of the life you're working toward.

Example

If you aim to improve your health, visualize yourself as energetic, confident, and active. Picture the freedom of a healthy body, the pride in maintaining discipline, and the joy of being able to do all the things you love. Let this vision become a source of strength as you work on building healthy habits.

Your "Why" as Your Anchor

Your "why" is the foundation of every meaningful goal. It's the anchor that keeps you steady when life gets challenging, the compass that guides your decisions, and the fuel that powers your journey. As you continue through this book, keep your "why" close—it will remind you why each step matters and keep you moving forward.

The next chapter will build on this foundation by transforming your purpose into specific, actionable goals. With a strong "why" as your guide, you're ready to set goals that feel both meaningful and achievable.

* * * *

Action Steps

Before Writing your "why" in one clear sentence, keep it visible—on a sticky note, in your journal, or on your phone. This reminder will keep you inspired as you pursue your dreams. With your "why" in place, it's time to turn purpose into action. In the next chapter, we'll explore how to set SMART goals—specific, measurable, achievable, relevant, and time-bound—and transform your vision into a clear, actionable plan.

Need help applying these strategies? Download the Vision to Victory Workbook for exercises, templates, and tools to guide you through every step.

2 SET SMART GOALS

Studies show that people who write down their goals are 42% more likely to achieve them. — Dr. Gail Matthews, Dominican University.

Setting goals is one of the most powerful tools for achieving success, but research reveals that clarity and structure are essential to making those goals a reality. In a landmark study, Dr. Gail Matthews found that people who wrote down their goals, created specific action steps, and shared progress with an accountability partner were up to 76% more likely to accomplish them. Turning vague ideas into specific, written goals engages our brain's problem-solving regions, making planning, focusing, and staying motivated easier. This is backed by goal-setting theory from researchers like Edwin Locke and Gary Latham, who found that specific and challenging goals lead to higher performance 90% of the time, compared to vague or easy goals.

The SMART framework—Specific, Measurable, Achievable, Relevant, and Time-bound—builds on these findings by creating a structure that enhances clarity, accountability, and focus. Studies show that people with well-defined goals and deadlines are significantly more likely to stay on track, while time-bound goals stimulate the brain's reward system, releasing dopamine each time we progress. In this chapter, we'll dive into each part of the SMART framework, explore how to set stretch goals for extra motivation and break down big goals into manageable steps. By the end, you'll have an actionable, well-structured plan that brings your vision closer to reality, helping you turn your dreams into achievable steps forward.

2.1 THE SMART FRAMEWORK

SMART stands for Specific, Measurable, Achievable, Relevant, and Time-bound. Introduced by George T. Doran in 1981, the SMART framework offers a structured method for setting goals. Each component helps transform vague intentions into clear, actionable steps, making your goals more focused and attainable. Let's break down each part with a sample goal to see it in action.

S – Specific: A specific goal clearly defines your goal. The more precise you are, the easier it is to create a plan. Avoid vague goals like "get in shape" or "be successful." Instead, focus on precisely what you want to achieve.

Example

- Vague goal: "Get in shape."
- Specific goal: "Run a 6K race in three months."

Exercise

Write down a goal that's important to you. Then ask yourself: Is this goal specific enough? If not, add more detail. What exactly are you aiming for?

M – Measurable: A measurable goal allows you to track your progress. Defining metrics lets you see how far you've come and stay motivated. Measurements can be quantitative (e.g., numbers, percentages) or qualitative (e.g., a personal rating scale).

Example

- Specific goal: "Run a 6K race in three months."
- Measurable goal: "Run a 6K race in under 60 minutes."

Exercise

Think about how you will measure your progress. Write down a metric for each goal that shows you are making headway. This could be a deadline, a target number, or a progress indicator.

A – Achievable: An achievable goal is realistic, given your current resources, skills, and timeframe. While it's essential to challenge yourself, setting too ambitious goals can lead to frustration and burnout. Consider whether you have the tools and support needed or need to acquire new skills or resources.

Example

- **Measurable goal:** "Run a 6K race in under 60 minutes."
- **Achievable goal:** "Run a 6K race in under 60 minutes after following a three-month training plan."

Exercise

Assess your goal for achievability. Do I have the skills, resources, and time to accomplish this goal? If not, what additional support or preparation would make it achievable?

R—Relevant: A relevant goal aligns with your broader vision and values. It should feel meaningful and serve a purpose in your life. Ask yourself how this goal connects to your long-term vision or core values (as explored in Chapter 1); if it doesn't align with your "why," you may need to adjust it.

Example

- **Achievable goal**: "Run a 6K race in under 60 minutes after following a three-month training plan."
- **Relevant goal:** "Run a 6K to improve my fitness, feel more energetic, and set a positive example for my family."

Exercise

Consider the relevance of each goal. Ask yourself: Does this goal align with my values and vision? Write down a brief statement of how achieving this goal will contribute to your life and connect with your deeper "why."

T – Time-bound: A time-bound goal has a clear deadline, which adds a sense of urgency and helps you stay focused. Setting a timeframe also allows you to break down your goal into manageable milestones so that you can keep track of your progress.

Example

- **Relevant goal:** "Run a 6K to improve my fitness, feel more energetic, and set a positive example for my family."
- **Time-bound goal:** "Run a 6K in under 60 minutes by April 15th, three months from now."

Exercise

Decide on a deadline for each of your goals. Please write it down and mark it on your calendar. If the goal is long-term, consider setting intermediate deadlines to track your progress.

2.2 Stretch Goals for Extra Motivation

SMART goals are great for creating structure, but sometimes, you need an extra push to stay motivated—especially for big, challenging dreams. This is where stretch goals come in. A stretch goal is an ambitious target that pushes you slightly beyond your comfort zone. It should feel exciting and challenging without being so unrealistic that it becomes discouraging.

Stretch goals help you grow by encouraging you to reach beyond what you initially thought was possible. They keep you motivated by adding excitement and reminding you of your potential.

Example

Let's say your SMART goal is to save $10,000 this year. A stretch goal might be to save $12,000 or even $15,000. The stretch goal challenges you to find additional ways to save or earn more money, pushing you to go further than your original plan.

Exercise: Set a Stretch Goal

- **Identify Your SMART Goal:** Review the SMART goals you've written down.
- **Consider How to Stretch It:** Expanding this goal slightly beyond what feels comfortable. It should be ambitious but still realistic. For

example, if your SMART goal is to complete a 6K in under 60 minutes, your stretch goal might be to run it in under 28 minutes.

- **Commit to Trying:** Write down your stretch goal and remind yourself that this is a target to strive for, not an absolute requirement. The purpose is to challenge yourself, not to add pressure.

By setting stretch goals, you can achieve even more than you initially planned, adding motivation and excitement to your journey.

2.3 BREAK BIG GOALS INTO SUBGOALS

Significant goals can feel overwhelming. When a goal seems too big, it's easy to procrastinate or feel paralyzed, unsure of where to start. Breaking big goals into smaller, manageable subgoals makes them achievable and gives you a clear path forward. Each small win builds momentum, reinforcing your commitment and helping you stay on track.

Example

Suppose your goal is to write a book in one year. That's a big goal, but breaking it into smaller parts makes it feel manageable. You might break it down like this:

- **Monthly Goal:** Write one chapter per month.

- **Weekly Goal:** Write five pages per week.
- **Daily Goal:** Write for 30 minutes each day.

By breaking the goal into smaller steps, you create a clear roadmap. This approach makes the goal less intimidating and helps you track progress and celebrate small wins.

Exercise: Create Subgoals

- **Choose a Large Goal:** Pick one of your SMART goals that feels ambitious or long-term.
- **Break It Down by Time:**
    - **Yearly Goal:** What's the main target you want to achieve by the end of the year?
    - **Monthly Goals:** Break it down into 12 smaller steps, each achievable within a month.
    - **Weekly Goals:** Identify the steps you must complete weekly to meet your monthly goals.
    - **Daily Actions:** Define small actions you can take daily to move toward your weekly goals.
- **Write It Down:** Include your subgoals in a journal or planner. This breakdown will be a checklist, helping you stay organized and focused on each step.

Example

If your goal is to improve your fitness, you could break it down like this:

- **Yearly Goal:** Lose 24 pounds and build muscle.
- **Monthly Goals:** Set a monthly target (e.g., lose 2 pounds, increase strength training).
- **Weekly Goals:** Complete four workouts, meal prep on Sundays, and track calorie intake daily.
- **Daily Actions**: Spend 30 minutes working out, drink a specific amount of water, and track meals.

Breaking big goals into smaller steps keeps you motivated and allows you to focus on one step at a time without feeling overwhelmed.

Turning Your Vision into Action

With SMART goals in place, you now have a clear and actionable plan to guide your efforts. Each step is purposeful, measurable, and achievable, creating a solid foundation for success. By adding stretch goals and breaking down big dreams into smaller steps, you've built a structure that will keep you motivated and focused as you move forward.

No matter how small, every action brings you closer to your dreams. Remember, success isn't one giant leap but consistent, intentional steps over time. With each goal you accomplish, you're reinforcing your commitment and building confidence in your ability to reach even higher.

In the next chapter, we'll take your vision one step further by crafting a personal vision statement to guide your journey. Let's keep moving toward your best self and your biggest dreams.

* * * *

Action Step

Take a moment to review your SMART goals, stretch goals, and subgoals. Write down a few thoughts on how it feels to have a clear plan. Do you feel more motivated? What excites you about the journey ahead?

Now that you have a structured plan with SMART goals, it's time to deepen your connection to your vision. In the next chapter, we'll work on crafting a personal vision statement—a powerful reminder of where you're headed and why it matters. Let's continue building the foundation for your success.

Need help applying these strategies? Download the Vision to Victory Workbook and refer to Chapter 2 for exercises, templates, and tools to guide you through every step.

3   CRAFT A VISION

Imagine waking up 10 years from now, staring at a life that feels unrecognizable—a life that somehow drifted far from the dreams you once held dear. You wonder how it happened. How did you get here? What decisions or distractions caused your goals to slip away? Perhaps you focused on the urgent rather than the important. Perhaps you hesitated, waiting for the "right time" to pursue your dreams. Those dreams feel like distant memories, replaced by a quiet regret.

But what if things were different? What if, instead of drifting aimlessly, you had a clear vision—a roadmap that aligned you with the life you truly wanted? Imagine living with purpose, with every decision, every step, and every choice guided by an unwavering sense of direction. How empowering would it be to know that you are moving closer to the life you envision for yourself each day?

A clear vision acts as that compass, ensuring you stay on course no matter how turbulent life becomes. It's more than just a wishful thought or a vague hope—it's a vivid, purposeful picture of the future that excites and energizes you. Your vision is the fire that keeps you motivated on the hard days and the light that shows you the way when the road ahead feels unclear.

Crafting a meaningful vision becomes your personal North Star, a constant guide that keeps you focused on what truly matters. It's not just about dreaming big; it's about anchoring those dreams to daily actions and aligning your decisions with your deepest values and aspirations. A well-defined vision inspires discipline, builds resilience, and gives you a powerful sense of clarity in a world of distractions.

In this chapter, we will explore how to create a vision that inspires you, motivates you, and keeps you moving forward—even when the path gets tough. You will learn what makes an outstanding vision statement, the steps to crafting your own, and how to bring that vision to life through intentional action. Together, we'll create a roadmap to the future you have always dreamed of and ensure that your vision serves as a guide to transform your life.

3.1 WHAT MAKES A GREAT VISION STATEMENT

A vision statement vividly describes the future you want to create. It should be ambitious yet realistic, inspiring yet grounded in your values and purpose. A great vision statement does more than outline a goal—it paints a picture of the life you aspire to live. When crafted effectively, it provides clarity, motivation, and a sense of purpose. A strong vision statement has three essential qualities:

- **Clarity:** It clearly articulates what you want your future to look like. Vague ideas like "I want to be successful" don't provide direction. A clear vision statement outlines specific elements of your ideal life so you know exactly what you're working toward.
- **Inspiration:** Your vision should resonate emotionally, excite you, and feel deeply meaningful. A vision without emotional impact won't sustain your motivation during difficult times.
- **Alignment with Values:** A vision statement that aligns with your values feels authentic and fulfilling. When your vision reflects your core beliefs, it keeps you grounded, even when external circumstances change.

Example

Consider a person who values creativity, independence, and family. Their vision statement might look like this:

"In ten years, I see myself running a successful creative business that allows me the freedom to work from anywhere. I balance my career with quality time for my family, and I have the financial freedom to travel and explore new cultures. My days are filled with meaningful work that challenges me, and I am constantly growing professionally and personally."

This vision statement is clear, inspiring, and aligned with the person's values. It provides a powerful mental image guiding their decisions and actions over the next decade.

Exercise

Think about what qualities make a great vision statement. What words or images come to mind when you imagine your ideal life? Jot down a few ideas that resonate with you. This exercise will help you lay the foundation for crafting an authentic and motivating vision statement.

3.2 STEPS TO CRAFT YOUR VISION

Crafting a vision is a reflective process. It requires you to look inward, reflect on what matters most, and dream without limitations. Here's a step-by-step guide to creating a vision statement that captures the future you want to build.

Step 1 - Reflect on Your Core Values and Priorities: Start by thinking about your core values—the principles that guide your life. These values will shape the vision you create, ensuring it feels true to who you are. Ask yourself:

- What do I value most in life? (Examples: freedom, creativity, health, family, financial security, adventure)
- What brings me the most joy and fulfillment?
- What kind of legacy do I want to leave?

Write down your top values and priorities. These will serve as the foundation of your vision statement and align with what matters most to you.

Step 2 - Imagine Your Ideal Future: Now, visualize yourself 5, 10, or even 20 years from now. Picture what your life would look like if everything went according to plan—if you achieved your biggest dreams and became the best version of yourself. Consider these questions:

- Where am I living? (Describe your surroundings, city or country, home environment.)
- What am I doing for work or career? (Are you an entrepreneur, a leader, or a creative professional?)
- Who am I with? (Are you surrounded by family, friends, colleagues, or a partner?)
- What does a typical day look like? (What are your routines, and how do you spend your time?)
- What am I passionate about? (What causes, hobbies, or interests drive you?)

Close your eyes and let yourself dream. After a few minutes, write down everything you saw and felt. Don't worry about editing—capture the vision in as much detail as possible.

Step 3 - Condense and Clarify: Review your notes and look for themes. Is there a central idea or emotion that stands out? Try to condense your vision into a few sentences that capture its essence. Please keep it simple, clear, and inspiring.

Example

"In 10 years, I am a thriving entrepreneur, living in a beautiful, inspiring place that allows me to balance work and personal life. I dedicate my time to projects that align with my values, spending quality time with family, and giving back to my community. My life is filled with growth, passion, and purpose."

This statement is concise but mighty, providing a clear direction for the future.

Step 4 - Refine and Personalize: Your vision statement should feel deeply personal. It is okay if it takes time to get it just right. Refine the language, remove anything that feels forced, and focus on what truly resonates with you. Make sure your vision feels like a goal worth pursuing.

Exercise

Read your vision statement out loud. How does it make you feel? If it excites you, brings you a sense of purpose, or gives you a surge of motivation, you are on the right track. If not, go back and make adjustments until it feels inspiring.

3.3 Bringing Your Vision to Life

Crafting a vision is only the beginning; the real work comes in bringing it to life. Your vision is a guide, but you must align your daily actions with this bigger picture to make it real. Here are a few ways to keep your vision alive and at the forefront of everything you do.

Break Your Vision Down into Milestones: A vision can feel overwhelming if you view it as one massive goal. Instead, break it down into milestones—specific, achievable steps that will bring you closer to your ideal life. For example, if your vision involves owning a business, start with milestones like:

- Researching and brainstorming business ideas
- Creating a business plan
- Building an initial network or client base
- Launching your first product or service

Milestones make your vision manageable and give you clear steps to work toward.

Create Daily and Weekly Habits that Support Your Vision: Consistency is critical to realizing your vision. Identify small habits you can incorporate into your daily or weekly routine that align with your long-term vision. Commit to regular exercise and meal planning if health and fitness are part of your vision. Suppose your vision includes financial freedom. Set up a habit of tracking expenses and budgeting.

Over time, these small habits compound, helping you move toward your vision without feeling overwhelmed.

Use Visualization Techniques to Reinforce Your Vision: Visualization is a powerful tool for keeping your vision vivid and real. Take a few minutes daily to close your eyes and mentally picture yourself living your ideal life. Imagine the details, feel the emotions, and let yourself experience the joy of that future. This practice strengthens your connection to your vision and helps you stay motivated, especially during challenging times.

Exercise

- Take five minutes to visualize your ideal future every morning or evening.

- Picture the setting, the people, the emotions, and the accomplishments.
- Let this mental imagery inspire you to take one small action that aligns with your daily vision.

Create a Vision Board: A vision board visually represents your goals and dreams. Collect images, quotes, and words representing your vision, and arrange them on a board or digital platform where you can see them daily. This constant reminder reinforces your commitment and keeps you focused on your long-term goals.

Your Vision as Your Compass

Your vision is the compass that guides every step you take. It is the reason behind each goal you set and the motivation that keeps you moving forward. With a clear and inspiring vision statement, you'll stay focused and resilient no matter what life throws your way. Whenever you face uncertainty or setbacks, return to your vision—it's your North Star, the anchor that reminds you of the future you're working to create.

Now that you have a clear direction, it's time to build the habits and routines to keep you moving toward your vision daily. In the next chapter, we'll explore how small, intentional habits can bring your dreams to life and help you consistently progress with every step.

****

Action Steps

Write your vision statement on a piece of paper or in your journal. Place it somewhere visible—as a reminder on your mirror, desk, or phone's home screen.

Please take a few moments each day to read it, reconnect with it, and let it guide your actions.

With a powerful vision guiding you, the next step is establishing habits that align with your dreams. In the following chapter, we will explore building daily routines that make progress feel natural and consistent. Let's take the next step toward crafting a life that reflects your highest aspirations.

Need help applying these strategies? Download the Vision to Victory Workbook and refer to Chapter 3 for more exercises, templates, and tools to guide you through every step.

4 BUILD HABITS

What if just two minutes a day could change your life?

When we think about transforming our lives, we often picture massive, overwhelming efforts—spending hours at the gym daily, cramming late into the night to master a new skill, or working tirelessly toward an ambitious goal. These grand gestures feel exciting at first but quickly become unsustainable. Truthfully, life-changing transformations don't come from occasional bursts of effort. They come from the quiet power of small, consistent actions repeated over time.

Imagine this: Instead of committing to a grueling one-hour workout daily, you start with just two minutes of stretching. Instead of trying to read an entire book in one sitting, you read just one page before bed. Instead of overhauling your daily routine, you begin by drinking a single glass of water each morning. These tiny actions may seem insignificant initially, but they are vital to building solid habits.

Small habits compound over time, creating a ripple effect that produces extraordinary results. This principle is backed by science. Research shows that habits are formed through repetition, and starting small makes it easier to stay consistent. By beginning with tiny actions, you lower the barrier to entry, build momentum, and create a foundation for lasting change. It's not about how considerable your initial effort is; it's about showing up every day, no matter how small the step may seem.

The beauty of small habits is that they grow naturally. Two minutes of stretching can turn into an entire workout routine. Writing a single sentence can blossom into a daily journaling habit. Small wins give you a sense of accomplishment, creating a feedback loop that motivates you to keep going. Over time, these small actions don't just change your behaviors—they change your identity. You begin to see yourself as someone who takes action, follows through, and moves steadily toward your goals.

In this chapter, we'll dive into the science behind habits and explore why they're powerful drivers of change. You'll learn about the Habit Loop—the cycle of cue, routine, and reward that governs every habit you form—and how to use it to your advantage. We'll discuss the 2-Minute Rule, a simple technique for starting habits so small they're almost impossible to fail at. Finally, we'll explore how tracking your progress can help you stay consistent and build long-term momentum.

What if you could change your life without the pressure of grand, sweeping gestures? What if just two minutes a day were enough to put you on the path to your biggest dreams? By the end of this chapter, you'll have the tools to turn even the most minor actions into habits that transform your life—one day at a time.

4.1 THE HABIT LOOP

Habits are automatic behaviors that develop through repetition and play a massive role in shaping our lives. Psychologists call the structure of a habit the Habit Loop, which consists of three main components: the cue, the routine, and the reward. Understanding the Habit Loop allows us to build new habits intentionally and break old ones that no longer serve us.

- **The Cue:** The cue is the trigger that initiates the habit. It could be a specific time of day, an emotional state, or something in your environment. For example, seeing your running shoes by the door might cue you to go for a jog, or feeling stressed might cue you to reach for a snack.
- **The Routine:** The routine is your actual behavior, the habit itself. For instance, after seeing your running shoes (cue), you go for a 10-minute jog (routine). This routine can be as simple or complex as you make it, but consistency is critical. When the routine follows the cue regularly, it starts to become automatic.

- **The Reward:** The reward is what you gain from completing the routine. This could be a sense of accomplishment, a burst of energy, or even a dopamine release in the brain. Rewards reinforce the habit by making it something your brain wants to repeat. Over time, the brain associates the cue with the reward, strengthening the Habit Loop and making the behavior feel automatic.

Example

Let's say you want to build a reading habit. Here's how a Habit Loop for reading might look:

- **Cue:** You finish dinner.
- **Routine:** You read for 10 minutes.
- **Reward:** You enjoy learning something new and unwinding after a long day.

Repeating this loop consistently makes reading after dinner an automatic part of your day. By understanding and intentionally designing the Habit Loop, you can build any habit you want, one small step at a time.

Exercise

Think about a habit you want to build. Identify a cue you could use to trigger this habit, a simple and manageable routine, and a reward that makes the habit enjoyable.

Write down your Habit Loop in three parts: Cue, Routine, and Reward.

4.2 THE 2-MINUTE RULE

One of the biggest challenges in building new habits is getting started. We often set ambitious goals—working out for an hour, meditating for 20 minutes, or writing an entire book chapter—and then struggle to maintain the energy and motivation to keep up. The 2-Minute Rule is a simple, effective way to overcome this barrier. It's based on the idea that any new habit should start with an action that takes two minutes or less.

The beauty of the 2-Minute Rule is that it makes starting easy. Reducing a habit to something you can do quickly lowers the mental resistance to getting started. Over time, this small action becomes the foundation for a more significant habit.

How the 2-Minute Rule Works?

The 2-Minute Rule involves breaking down your desired habit into a "gateway action"—a small, easy step you can complete in under two minutes. The purpose is not necessarily to accomplish the entire habit but to build the momentum that makes continuing easier.

Examples

Here are some examples of how you can apply the 2-Minute Rule to different habits:

- Want to start exercising? Just put on your workout clothes. Once you're dressed, it's easier to follow through.
- Want to start reading more? Commit to reading one page a day. Often, you'll find yourself wanting to read more.
- Want to start writing a book? Write one sentence. Once you start, you are likely to continue.
- Want to meditate regularly? Sit down, close your eyes, and take a few deep breaths. You are building the habit even if you meditate for just a minute.

The key to the 2-minute Rule is that it eliminates the pressure of the more enormous task. Starting with a small action creates momentum, making it easier to build on that habit over time.

Exercise

Think about the habit you want to build. What is a 2-minute version of that habit? Write down this "gateway action" and commit to it daily. Remember, the goal is to get started—anything beyond the 2-minute action is a bonus.

4.3 TRACK YOUR PROGRESS

Once you have established a habit, tracking your progress is essential for staying consistent and motivated. When you track a habit, you create a visual record of your commitment, making it harder to miss a day and more accessible to recognize your progress over time. Even the slightest progress, when tracked, can create a powerful sense of accomplishment.

There are many ways to track your habits, and you can choose the one that feels most motivating to you:

1. **Habit Tracking Apps:** Numerous apps make habit tracking simple and fun. Apps like Habitica, Streaks, and HabitBull allow you to check off each day you complete your habit, providing visual feedback on your progress. Many apps also send reminders to help you stay consistent.
2. **Physical Habit Trackers:** If you prefer something tangible, try using a physical habit tracker. This could be a simple calendar where you mark off each day you complete your habit or even a habit journal where you record your thoughts and reflections. Seeing a string of successful days on a calendar can be highly motivating.
3. **The "Don't Break the Chain" Method:** Made famous by comedian Jerry Seinfeld, the "Don't

Break the Chain" method is a straightforward and effective way to build consistency. Each day you complete your habit, mark an X on a calendar. Your goal is to keep the chain going without breaking it. Over time, the desire to maintain the streak motivates you to stay consistent.

Exercise

Pick a method that appeals to you—a habit-tracking app, a calendar, or a journal—and commit to tracking your progress for at least 30 days. Remember, the goal isn't perfection; it's consistency. Every day you complete your habit, you reinforce the behavior and move closer to your long-term goals.

Why Tracking Matters

Tracking isn't just about accountability—it's also about celebrating small wins. Each time you check off a day or mark a completed habit, your brain receives a hit of dopamine, the "feel-good" chemical. This reward system reinforces the habit, making you more likely to repeat the behavior. Celebrating small wins, no matter how minor they seem, creates a positive feedback loop that fuels your motivation.

Example

Imagine your goal is to write every day. Each time you track a day of writing, you reinforce that behavior in your brain. You start associating writing with a feeling of accomplishment. As the habit becomes more ingrained, you'll find it easier to sit down and write each day because your brain has learned to expect a reward.

Build Big Goals with Small Habits

Big goals are built on small, consistent habits. Even a tiny habit practiced daily can create a ripple effect that leads to profound change over time. Remember, the key to success isn't doing something massive—it's doing something consistently. The 2-minute Rule, the Habit Loop, and habit tracking make it easy to get started and stay on track. You're building a foundation for lasting change by taking daily small steps.

In the next chapter, we'll explore how to design powerful routines that make your habits stick even more effectively. By creating intentional routines, you can automate positive behaviors and build momentum toward your goals without thinking about it. Let's continue moving forward, one small habit at a time.

* * * *

Action Steps

Reflect on the habits you want to build and the small actions you can take each day. Write down one habit you'd like to track and commit to practicing it for at least 30 days. Remember, consistency is the secret to transformation. Every day you complete your habit, you are a step closer to becoming the person you want to become.

With your habits in place, it's time to look at how routines can make those habits even stronger. In the next chapter, we'll discuss how to design routines that support your goals and make progress feel effortless. By combining habits with intentional routines, you'll create a system of success that propels you toward your vision.

Need help applying these strategies? Download the Vision to Victory Workbook and refer to Chapter 4 for more exercises, templates, and tools to guide you through every step.

5 CREATE ROUTINES

What sets champions apart from the rest? Is it raw talent, luck, or something else entirely? For basketball legend Kobe Bryant, the answer was simple: relentless discipline and purposeful routines.

Kobe's early-morning ritual is one of the most inspiring examples of the power of routines. While many of his teammates were still asleep, Kobe was already on the court—practicing at 4 a.m. daily, year after year. For him, this wasn't just about logging extra hours of practice. It was about creating a structure that built focus, mental toughness, and an edge over the competition. His mornings became sacred, and he pushed himself beyond limits, preparing his body and mind for the challenges ahead. This dedication to his routine was a key factor propelling him to legendary status.

Now, you may not be training for an NBA championship, but Kobe's story offers a universal truth: routines are the foundation of greatness. They are more than just a way to manage your time—they are systems that shape your habits, amplify your focus, and align your actions with your goals. A well-designed routine creates consistency, and consistency is what transforms dreams into achievements.

Think about your own life for a moment. How do you begin your day? Is it rushed, reactive, and scattered? Or is it intentional, focused, and productive? How you start your morning often sets the tone for the rest of your day. Similarly, your evening routine is crucial in helping you reflect, reset, and recharge for the challenges ahead. When you take control of these routines, you take control of your time—and, ultimately, your results.

The beauty of routines is that they don't have to be complicated or rigid. The most effective routines are simple, flexible, and personalized to fit your goals and lifestyle. A great morning routine might include 10 minutes of journaling to clarify your intentions, a quick workout to energize your body, and a moment of gratitude to shift your mindset. An evening routine might involve reviewing your accomplishments, planning the next day, and disconnecting from screens to wind down. These small but purposeful actions, when repeated consistently, have a compounding effect on your success.

This chapter will explore the art and science of building routines that align with your goals and priorities. You'll learn how to craft powerful morning and evening routines that set you up for daily success, create goal-oriented checklists to stay organized and on track, and develop the flexibility needed to adjust your routines when life throws unexpected challenges.

Imagine waking up each morning with clarity, purpose, and a sense of control over your day. Picture ending each evening with the satisfaction of knowing you're making consistent progress toward your dreams. That's the power of routines—they turn chaos into structure, distraction into focus, and effort into results. By the end of this chapter, you'll have the tools to design your days with intention and create a foundation for success that supports you, no matter where life takes you.

5.1 Design Routines

Your morning and evening routines are the bookends of your day, setting the tone for productivity and helping you wind down effectively. While mornings are an opportunity to start the day with intention, evenings provide a chance to reflect, recharge, and prepare for tomorrow. A well-designed morning and evening routine can create momentum that keeps you focused, energized, and consistently working toward your goals.

Morning Routines

Starting the Day with Intention: How you start your day often determines how the rest will unfold. A powerful morning routine doesn't have to be long or complicated; it just needs to be intentional. It's about doing key activities that prime your mind and body for success. Elements of a Productive Morning Routines are:

- **Wake Up at a Consistent Time:** Consistency in your wake-up time trains your body's internal clock, helping you feel more alert and energized each morning. Set a time that works for you and stick to it, even on weekends.
- **Practice Mindfulness or Gratitude:** Take a few moments to breathe deeply, meditate, or practice gratitude. This will set a positive tone and help you focus on the present. Studies show that gratitude practices can improve mental health and increase resilience.
- **Move Your Body:** Physical activity, even a quick stretch or short walk, boosts energy levels and improves focus. Exercise releases endorphins, helping you feel more positive and alert.
- **Review Your Goals or Set Intentions for the Day:** Take a few minutes to review your daily goals or set intentions for the day. This will align your focus with your long-term vision and ensure your actions are purposeful.
- **Eat a Healthy Breakfast:** Fueling your body with nutritious food provides the energy you need to tackle the day. Avoid heavy or sugary foods that may cause energy crashes later.

Example

- 6:30 a.m. – Wake up, stretch, and drink water.
- 6:40 a.m. – Spend 5 minutes in meditation or gratitude journaling.
- 6:50 a.m. – Do a 20-minute workout or brisk walk outside.
- 7:15 a.m. – Review daily goals and set an intention for the day.
- 7:20 a.m. – Have a balanced breakfast, such as oatmeal with fruits and nuts.

Exercise

Think about the elements you'd like to include in your morning routine. Write down a simple plan that fits your lifestyle, remembering that the goal is consistency, not perfection. Try to stick with it for a week and make adjustments as needed.

Evening Routines

Reflecting and Recharging: An evening routine helps you wind down, reflect on the day's progress, and prepare for a productive tomorrow. Ending your day intentionally allows you to go to bed with a clear mind, improving the quality of your sleep and setting you up for success the next day. Elements of an Effective Evening Routine are:

- **Review the Day:** Reflect on your accomplishments and consider any challenges you faced. Acknowledge your wins, no matter how small, and note any lessons learned.
- **Plan for Tomorrow:** Review your schedule for the next day and identify your top priorities. This will give you a head start and reduce decision fatigue in the morning.
- **Unplug and Disconnect:** Reduce screen time at least 30 minutes before bed. Blue light from devices can interfere with sleep quality, so consider reading a book or relaxing instead.
- **Practice Relaxation Techniques:** Whether it's deep breathing, gentle stretching, or a few minutes of meditation, relaxation techniques help your body and mind wind down, improving the quality of your rest.
- **Set a Consistent Bedtime:** Going to bed at the same time every night improves your sleep quality and makes it easier to wake up consistently.

Example

- 9:00 p.m. – Review the day and reflect on your achievements.
- 9:10 p.m. – Write a to-do list or set priorities for tomorrow.

- 9:20 p.m. – Read a book or journal to unwind.
- 9:30 p.m. – Practice a few minutes of deep breathing or stretching.
- 9:45 p.m. – Go to bed.

Exercise

Design a simple evening routine that helps you relax and prepare for the next day. Keep it realistic and enjoyable, focusing on activities that help you unwind and reflect.

5.2 GOAL CHECKLISTS

Checklists are powerful tools for maintaining focus and completing essential tasks. Creating a goal-oriented checklist allows you to break down larger goals into manageable steps, ensuring that each day's actions align with your broader vision. Following are the benefits of Using Checklists:

1. **Clarity and Focus:** Checklists help you stay organized and avoid feeling overwhelmed. They provide a clear path of action, making it easier to focus on one task at a time.
2. **Increased Productivity:** A checklist breaks tasks into smaller, achievable steps, which boosts productivity. You are likelier to complete small tasks than tackle one big, vague project.

3. **Sense of Accomplishment:** Checking off items as you complete them provides a sense of accomplishment, which boosts motivation. Each completed task is a small win that reinforces your progress.

Example

If your goal is to write a book, a daily checklist might look like this:

- Outline critical points for the next chapter.
- Write 500 words.
- Review yesterday's writing for edits.
- Spend 15 minutes brainstorming ideas.

You create a clear structure that keeps you focused and productive by breaking your goal into daily tasks. The checklist is a roadmap for achieving your goal, one small step at a time.

Exercise

Choose a specific goal you're working on. Break it into small, actionable steps to add to your daily or weekly checklist. Make it a habit to review and update your checklist regularly, ensuring it aligns with your current priorities.

5.3 CREATE FLEXIBILITY

While routines provide structure, it's essential to build flexibility. Life is unpredictable, and rigid routines can lead to stress or frustration if things don't go as planned. Flexible routines allow you to adapt without losing momentum, ensuring you can stay on track with your goals even when life throws you a curveball. Following are the tips for creating a flexible routine:

1. **Set Priorities:** Identify your top daily priorities and focus on completing those first. Even if something unexpected comes up, you'll still have completed the most critical tasks.
2. **Use Time Blocks:** Rather than scheduling specific tasks at rigid times, use time blocks for different types of activities (e.g., "work block" or "exercise block"). This approach gives you flexibility in when you complete tasks within each block.
3. **Have a "Backup Routine":** Create a shorter, simplified version of your routine for days when you're short on time. For example, if your regular morning routine includes a 30-minute workout, your backup routine might be a quick 5-minute stretch.
4. **Practice Self-Compassion:** Allow yourself some grace if you occasionally deviate from your

routine. Remember, routines are tools to support your goals, not rigid rules that you must follow perfectly.

Example of a Flexible Morning Routine

- o **Primary Routine**: Wake up, meditate, exercise for 20 minutes, review goals, and have breakfast.
- o **Backup Routine (for busy days)**: Wake up, do 5 minutes, review goals quickly, and grab a light breakfast.

This flexibility ensures that even on challenging days, you can still engage with your routine in some form, keeping up your momentum without the pressure of perfection.

Exercise

Look at your morning or evening routine and identify areas where you could add flexibility. Create a backup version of your routine to stay on track even on busy or unpredictable days.

The Power of Consistent Routines

A good routine takes the guesswork out of your day and keeps you on track to achieve your goals. Routines provide structure and efficiency, allowing you to focus on what truly matters. But routines aren't just about discipline—they can also create space for growth, creativity, and self-care. By building flexibility into your routines, you can adapt to life's changes without losing sight of your goals.

Keep refining and personalizing your routines as you move forward until they feel natural and supportive. In the next chapter, we'll tackle one of the biggest enemies of progress: procrastination—and explore strategies to overcome it so you can stay committed to your vision.

* * * *

Action Steps

Take a moment to reflect on your routines. Are they supporting your goals, or do they need adjustment? Write down one change you could make to strengthen your morning or evening routine and commit to trying it for the next week.

With effective routines in place, the next challenge is to overcome procrastination—the silent barrier that often holds us back. In the next chapter, we'll explore practical techniques for beating procrastination and staying consistent in working toward your dreams.

Need help applying these strategies? Download the Vision to Victory Workbook and refer to Chapter 5 for more exercises, templates, and tools to guide you through every step.

6   BEAT PROCRASTINATION

Have you ever sat down to tackle something important—a work project, a personal goal, or even a simple task like organizing your desk—only to find yourself scrolling endlessly through Instagram, checking your inbox for the fifth time that hour, or wandering into the kitchen to grab a snack you didn't even want? Maybe the clock is ticking, the deadline is looming, and you know you should get started, but you can't bring yourself to do it. Instead, you feel stuck, distracted, and even frustrated with yourself. Sound familiar? Don't worry—you're not alone.

Procrastination is one of the most common hurdles we face, and we've all experienced it at one point or another. It sneaks up on us in moments when we need to focus most, pulling us away from meaningful action and into a spiral of avoidance and guilt. We delay starting, telling ourselves we'll feel more motivated later, only to find ourselves further behind and even more overwhelmed. While it's easy to blame procrastination on laziness or a lack of willpower, the truth is much more complex: procrastination is a learned behavior—a coping mechanism rooted in emotion, fear, and habit.

Why do we procrastinate? Often, it's not because we are lazy or incapable but because we are avoiding something uncomfortable. Maybe the task feels too big or too uncertain. Maybe we are afraid of failure—or even success. Perhaps we are overwhelmed by perfectionism or paralyzed by where to begin. Procrastination is our brain's way of protecting us from discomfort, but in doing so, it becomes a barrier that keeps us from reaching our potential. It's one of the biggest reasons why goals are left unachieved, dreams are postponed, and confidence is eroded.

The good news is that procrastination is just a habit; like any habit, it can be understood, broken, and replaced with more productive behaviors. The first step is recognizing procrastination for what it is: a pattern, not a personality trait. Once you see it clearly, you can begin to take control of it.

This chapter will explore the psychology behind procrastination and uncover the triggers that lead to avoidance. You'll learn how to identify the emotional and mental blocks that hold you back so you can address them head-on. We'll introduce practical, proven strategies to help you stop procrastination, including the 5-Second Rule, a simple yet powerful method for taking immediate action, and task-chunking, a technique to make overwhelming projects feel manageable and achievable.

Imagine being able to sit down and start working on a big project without hesitation. Picture yourself no longer feeling weighed down by unfinished tasks or distracted by endless scrolling. By the end of this chapter, you'll have the tools to break free from the procrastination cycle and take meaningful, consistent action toward your goals. Procrastination doesn't have to hold you back anymore—it's time to reclaim your focus, rebuild your momentum, and move confidently in the direction of your dreams.

6.1 PROCRASTINATION TRIGGERS

To beat procrastination, it's essential to understand why it happens in the first place. Procrastination isn't usually about laziness; it's often rooted in deeper psychological factors like fear of failure, perfectionism, or simply feeling overwhelmed by the size of the task. When we can identify the triggers that lead to procrastination, we can counteract them effectively.

Common Procrastination Triggers

1. **Fear of Failure:** When a task feels challenging or intimidating, we may avoid it out of fear that we won't succeed. This fear can be paralyzing, leading us to postpone tasks to protect ourselves from potential disappointment.

2. **Perfectionism:** Some people procrastinate because they believe everything they do must be perfect. The fear of not meeting their high standards can stop them from starting.
3. **Overwhelming:** Large tasks or projects can feel daunting. When we look at the entirety of what needs to be done, it's easy to feel overwhelmed, leading to avoidance as a coping mechanism.
4. **Instant Gratification:** Our brains are wired to seek pleasure and avoid pain. When a task seems complicated, we're more likely to choose more leisurely, more enjoyable activities—like watching TV or scrolling on social media—that provide immediate gratification.
5. **Lack of Clarity:** Sometimes, we procrastinate simply because we don't know where to start. If a task is poorly defined, it's hard to take the first step.

Exercise

Take a moment to think about a task or goal you have avoided. Ask yourself which of these triggers might be holding you back. Write down any insights you have about why you're procrastinating. Understanding your triggers is the first step toward overcoming them.

6.2 TAKE ACTION BEFORE YOUR BRAIN STOPS

One of the most effective strategies for overcoming procrastination is the 5-Second Rule, popularized by motivational speaker Mel Robbins. The 5-Second Rule is simple but powerful: when you feel the urge to act on a goal, you count down—5, 4, 3, 2, 1—and then take action immediately. This technique works because it interrupts your brain's instinct to hesitate and slightly pushes you to start.

The science behind the 5-Second Rule lies in the way our brains work. When we hesitate, our brain's prefrontal cortex—responsible for decision-making—kicks in with all the reasons why we shouldn't act, leading us to procrastinate. By counting down from five and acting immediately, we bypass this hesitation response and take control.

How to Use the 5-Second Rule

1. **Identify the Action You Need to Take:** Consider the task or action you have avoided. It could be as simple as starting a report, sending an email, or getting up to exercise.
2. **Count down from 5:** As soon as you feel the hesitation, start counting down in your mind—5, 4, 3, 2, 1. Counting backward creates a sense of

urgency and interrupts any procrastination thoughts.

3. **Take Immediate Action:** When you reach "1," take immediate action. This doesn't have to mean finishing the entire task; it's about taking the first small step. If you're procrastinating on writing, open a blank document. If you're avoiding exercise, put on your workout shoes.

Example

Imagine you're procrastinating on starting a big presentation for work. When you feel that familiar dread or avoidance, count down—5, 4, 3, 2, 1—and open the presentation software. Type a title, add a few bullet points, or outline the first slide. Taking this small action helps you overcome the initial resistance, and often, you'll find it easier to keep going.

Exercise

Choose a task you've been putting off and use the 5-Second Rule to get started. Write down your action and how it felt to bypass the hesitation—practice using this technique regularly to build a habit of immediate action.

6.3 BREAK TASKS INTO CHUNKS

When a task feels overwhelming, it's easy to procrastinate. One of the best ways to tackle large, intimidating tasks is by breaking them down into smaller, manageable chunks. This approach, known as task chunking, makes big projects feel more achievable and helps you build momentum through small wins.

How to Break Down a Task

1. **Define the End Goal:** Clearly define your goal. Write down your end goal to give you a clear picture of the task.
2. **Break It into Smaller Steps:** Divide the task into smaller, specific steps. For example, if your goal is to write a report, break it down into steps like "research topic," "create an outline," "write an introduction," and so on.
3. **Focus on One Step at a Time:** Once you've broken down the task, focus only on the first small step. Instead of thinking about the entire report, concentrate on completing the outline. Once you finish that, move on to the next step.
4. **Set Micro-Deadlines:** Assign mini-deadlines for each chunk. Instead of setting one deadline for the whole task, give yourself specific timeframes for each step. This reduces the feeling of being overwhelmed and keeps you moving forward.

Example

Suppose you must clean and organize your entire garage—a daunting task. Start by breaking it into smaller steps:

- o Step 1: Sort items into "keep" and "donate" piles.
- o Step 2: Clean the floor and shelves.
- o Step 3: Organize tools and equipment.
- o Step 4: Label storage boxes.

Each step can be completed independently, and focusing on just one chunk at a time makes the whole project feel more manageable.

Exercise

Identify a goal or project that feels overwhelming. Please write down the steps needed to complete it and focus on completing the first step. Taking it one chunk at a time will reduce stress and ensure consistent progress.

Why These Strategies Work

Procrastination thrives on hesitation, overwhelm, and perfectionism. The strategies we've discussed in this chapter—identifying procrastination triggers, using the 5-Second Rule, and breaking tasks into chunks—are designed to counteract these barriers:

- Identifying triggers helps you understand why you procrastinate, empowering you to take proactive steps.

- The 5-Second Rule interrupts hesitation, getting you into action before your brain talks you out.
- Task chunking reduces overwhelm by breaking big projects into manageable steps, making starting and maintaining momentum easier.

By practicing these techniques regularly, you'll start to build a habit of action, replacing procrastination with progress.

Turning Procrastination into Productivity

Procrastination is just a habit—like any habit, it can be changed. By understanding your triggers, taking immediate action with the 5-Second Rule, and breaking tasks into smaller steps, you can stay ahead of procrastination and move consistently toward your goals. Remember, overcoming procrastination isn't about perfection; it's about creating a system that makes it easier to start and keep going.

Now that you're ready to take action let's look at how to plan and prioritize your tasks effectively in the next chapter. When you combine the power of planning with the skills you've learned here, you'll be unstoppable in achieving your dreams.

* * * *

Action Steps

Reflect on a recent task you procrastinated on. Identify which trigger might have caused the procrastination and choose one of the techniques in this chapter to apply to a similar task in the future. Write down how you plan to use the 5-Second Rule or task chunking to make starting easier.

With the tools to overcome procrastination, it's time to tackle planning and prioritization. In the next chapter, we'll explore practical methods for organizing your tasks, setting priorities, and ensuring your efforts focus on what truly matters. Let's take the next step in bringing your vision to life, one intentional action at a time.

Need help applying these strategies? Download the Vision to Victory Workbook and refer to Chapter 6 for more exercises, templates, and tools to guide you through every step.

7 Plan and Prioritize

What is the difference between people who achieve their goals and those who don't? It often boils down to one simple factor: having a plan with clear, specific deadlines. Research shows that setting deadlines can increase goal achievement by as much as 50%. That's the power of commitment. When you give yourself a timeline, you create urgency and accountability. You move from "someday" thinking to purposeful action. Without deadlines, even the most ambitious goals can fall victim to procrastination, distractions, or competing priorities.

Think about it—how often have you told yourself, "I'll start next week," or, "I'll get to it when I have more time"? Weeks turn into months; before you know it, the momentum has fizzled out, leaving your dreams untouched. Deadlines act as a force that propels you forward. They transform vague aspirations into actionable steps, helping you stay focused and motivated. A clear deadline signals to your brain that this goal matters and is time to act.

However, deadlines are only part of the equation. Success requires more than knowing when you'll achieve something—it requires knowing how to get there. That's where planning and prioritizing come in. Without a clear plan, even the most specific deadline can feel overwhelming. It's like embarking on a road trip without a map: you know where you want to go but are unsure of the best way. A good plan breaks your goal into manageable milestones, showing you exactly what steps to take and when. Each milestone becomes a checkpoint on your journey, keeping you on track and building momentum as you go.

Planning also requires prioritization. Only some tasks on your to-do list are equally important, and trying to do everything at once can leave you feeling overwhelmed and ineffective. This is where tools like the Eisenhower Matrix come into play. By distinguishing between urgent and truly important, you can focus your time and energy on the tasks with the most significant impact. Prioritization isn't just about doing more; it's about doing the right things at the right time.

This chapter will explore the art of effective planning and prioritization—two essential skills for turning your goals into reality. You'll learn to set milestones that break big goals into smaller, achievable chunks, creating a step-by-step roadmap for success. We'll dive into the Eisenhower Matrix, a powerful tool for sorting tasks by urgency and importance so you can focus on what truly matters. Finally, we'll introduce practical tools for tracking your progress, helping you stay organized and motivated as you progress.

Imagine having a clear roadmap for your dreams—knowing precisely what to do next, feeling in control of your time, and seeing consistent progress toward your goals. That's the power of planning and prioritization. By the end of this chapter, you'll have a system that helps you get organized and ensures that your daily actions align with your vision for the future. It's time to take control of your plans, prioritize what matters most, and confidently take the next step toward achieving your dreams.

7.1 Turn Big Goals into Manageable Steps

Setting a big, ambitious goal is exciting but can also feel overwhelming. One of the best ways to stay motivated and on track is to break down your goal into smaller, manageable steps called milestones. Each milestone serves as a mini-goal, bringing you closer to the larger objective while providing a sense of accomplishment.

Why Milestones Matter

Milestones help you maintain momentum by turning long-term goals into actionable steps. Instead of feeling like you're aiming for something far off, milestones allow you to focus on one step at a time. This approach makes the journey less daunting and helps you track your progress more effectively.

Example

Let's say your goal is to write a book in one year. This big goal might feel overwhelming, but breaking it into milestones makes it manageable. Here's what a milestone plan might look like:

- o Milestone 1: Complete the outline (End of Month 1)
- o Milestone 2: Write the first three chapters (End of Month 3)
- o Milestone 3: Reach the halfway point of the manuscript (End of Month 6)
- o Milestone 4: Finish the first draft (End of Month 9)
- o Milestone 5: Complete editing and revisions (End of Month 11)
- o Milestone 6: Submit the manuscript to publishers or self-publish (End of Month 12)

Focusing on each milestone rather than the entire book can help you maintain your motivation and keep moving forward.

Exercise

1. **Define Your End Goal:** Write down your big goal and set a target deadline for achieving it.
2. **Break It Down into Milestones:** Divide your goal into smaller steps or phases. Each milestone

should have a deadline that fits within the timeframe of your larger goal.
3. **Set Specific Deadlines:** Assign a specific date to each milestone. Research shows that setting deadlines improves goal achievement by making your plans concrete and time-bound.
4. **Celebrate Small Wins:** Each time you reach a milestone, take a moment to celebrate. This recognition reinforces your progress and keeps you motivated.

7.2 PRIORITIZING TASKS THAT MATTER

Knowing what to do is only half the battle when planning. Equally important is knowing what to prioritize. The Eisenhower Matrix, named after former U.S. President Dwight D. Eisenhower, is a simple yet powerful tool for prioritizing tasks based on urgency and importance. The Eisenhower Matrix divides tasks into four categories:

- o Quadrant 1: Urgent and Important
- o Quadrant 2: Not Urgent but Important
- o Quadrant 3: Urgent but Not Important
- o Quadrant 4: Not Urgent and Not Important

This matrix helps you identify which tasks require immediate attention and careful planning and which can be delegated or eliminated.

How to Use the Eisenhower Matrix

List Your Tasks: Start by writing down all the tasks you need to complete. This could include work projects, personal responsibilities, and anything else demanding your attention.

Sort Tasks by Urgency and Importance: Place each task into one of the four quadrants:

- **Quadrant 1** (Urgent and Important): Tasks that need immediate attention, like deadlines or emergencies.
- **Quadrant 2** (Not Urgent but Important): Long-term goals and planning, like working on a personal project or developing a new skill. These tasks are critical to progress but don't have immediate deadlines.
- **Quadrant 3** (Urgent but Not Important): Tasks that demand attention but don't contribute to your long-term goals, like some emails or interruptions. Delegate these when possible.
- **Quadrant 4** (Not Urgent and Not Important): Tasks that are distractions, like excessive social media or watching TV. Eliminate these whenever possible.

The tasks in Quadrant 2 (Not Urgent but Important) are where progress is made. These tasks often relate to personal growth, health, relationships, and long-term goals. Make time each day to work on at least one Quadrant 2 task.

Example

Imagine you're preparing for a major presentation at work. Here's how your tasks might fit into the matrix:

- o Quadrant 1: Finalize slides for tomorrow's meeting (Urgent and Important)
- o Quadrant 2: Research new data to support your presentation (Not Urgent but Important)
- o Quadrant 3: Respond to non-urgent emails from colleagues (Urgent but Not Important)
- o Quadrant 4: Scroll through social media (Not Urgent and Not Important)

By focusing on tasks in Quadrant 2 and managing or eliminating tasks in Quadrants 3 and 4, you can stay focused on what truly matters.

Exercise:

List out your current tasks and sort them into the Eisenhower Matrix. Identify at least one Quadrant 2 task you can work on today. Make it a habit to review your matrix regularly and adjust as needed.

7.3 STAYING ORGANIZED AND ON TRACK

Once you have set your milestones and prioritized your tasks, the next step is to find a system to keep everything organized. Tracking your progress ensures that nothing falls through the cracks and helps you stay motivated by showing you how far you've come. Here are some popular tools and methods for tracking your plans.

Digital Project Management Tools: Digital tools like Trello, Asana, and Notion are great for organizing tasks, setting deadlines, and tracking progress. These tools allow you to create each goal's boards, lists, and timelines. You can also set reminders, create checklists, and collaborate with others.

- **Trello** is best for visual learners who like organizing tasks on boards. You can create a board for each goal and add "cards" for each milestone or task.
- **Asana**: Great for managing complex projects with multiple deadlines. You can assign tasks to different categories and track each step.
- **Notion**: It is highly customizable, allowing you to create databases, checklists, and progress trackers that fit your workflow.

Bullet Journaling: If you prefer a physical approach, bullet journaling is a popular and flexible method for tracking your goals. You can design a bullet journal to include lists, monthly goals, daily tasks, and habit trackers. Bullet journaling allows you to keep all your plans in one place and customize the layout.

Example

You could create a monthly spread with milestones and weekly pages for daily tasks in your bullet journal. You can also add habit trackers, goal reflections, and monthly reviews to stay engaged with your progress.

Calendar-Based Tracking: A calendar-based approach can be highly effective for deadline-driven goals. Whether digital or physical, calendars allow you to set deadlines, block time for specific tasks, and visualize your progress over the month or year.

- **Digital Calendar:** Use Google Calendar or Outlook to set reminders for each milestone. Schedule specific work sessions for essential tasks.
- **Physical Calendar:** A wall calendar or planner lets you see your deadlines at a glance. Marking off each day you work toward your goal can also provide a sense of accomplishment.

Exercise

Try different tracking tools or methods to see which fits your style. Use them consistently for at least a month to see if they help you stay organized and motivated.

Why Planning and Prioritization Matter

Planning and prioritization are essential for translating your vision into actionable steps. Without a plan, goals can feel overwhelming and vague. Setting milestones, prioritizing effectively, and using tools to track your progress gives you the structure needed to stay on course.

Planning doesn't just organize your time; it provides a sense of direction. Prioritizing ensures that your efforts go toward tasks that genuinely matter, helping you avoid busy work and focus on meaningful progress. With these strategies, you can work on your goals efficiently, even when life gets hectic.

Making Consistent Progress

A great plan gives you direction, but prioritization ensures you make real progress. With the right strategy, you'll be able to focus on what truly matters without getting overwhelmed. Planning and prioritizing aren't one-time activities; they're ongoing processes that align you with your goals. You'll build a system that supports your success by setting clear milestones, prioritizing tasks with the Eisenhower Matrix, and tracking your progress.

In the next chapter, we'll explore the power of accountability and how it can keep you motivated even on the most challenging days. Accountability can be the extra push you need to stay on track, helping you follow through on your plans.

* * * *

Action Steps

Review your current goal and write down one milestone, identify a Quadrant 2 task that supports it, and choose a tracking method to stay organized. Your progress will feel more achievable with a solid plan and clear priorities. In the next chapter, we'll explore accountability—an essential factor in boosting commitment and staying motivated, even on tough days. Let's keep moving forward!

Need help applying these strategies? Download the Vision to Victory Workbook and refer to Chapter 7 for more exercises, templates, and tools to guide you through every step.

8 Stay Accountable

When Bill Gates co-founded Microsoft, he wasn't alone. His trusted partner, Paul Allen, was alongside him. Together, they navigated the highs and lows of building one of history's most successful technology companies. Their partnership wasn't just a division of labor—it was a powerful bond of mutual accountability. When Gates faced challenges, Allen was there to push him forward, and when Allen needed support, Gates was equally committed. They relied on each other to show up, contribute, and deliver. This sense of shared responsibility didn't just propel their work; it fueled their progress and gave them the discipline to pursue a bold vision with unwavering focus.

Gates and Allen's story demonstrates a truth that resonates far beyond the business world: accountability is a game-changer. Having someone in your corner— whether a partner, a mentor, or even a close friend— dramatically increases your chances of success. Why? Because accountability transforms your goals from private aspirations into shared commitments. When you share your goals with someone who believes in you, you're no longer just accountable to yourself; you have someone else invested in your success. This external motivation pushes you to keep going, even when you feel like giving up.

Think about it: How often do we break our promises to ourselves? It's easy to skip that workout, delay that project, or put off pursuing a dream when no one else knows about it. But when we're accountable to someone else—when we've told a friend, a coach, or a partner what we plan to achieve—it becomes much more challenging to back out. Accountability creates a sense of responsibility and urgency. It transforms "I'll get to it someday" into "I need to follow through because someone is counting on me."

Accountability isn't just about partnerships—it's about creating a support system that keeps you focused and consistent. This can take many forms: a one-on-one relationship with an accountability partner, a supportive group where you regularly share your progress, or even a public commitment that gives you the extra motivation to follow through. Involving others in your goals provides clarity, perspective, and encouragement. It also offers a safety net, ensuring you don't lose momentum when the road gets tough.

In this chapter, we'll dive into how you can use accountability to achieve your goals. You'll learn to find the right accountability partner or join a group that shares your ambitions. We'll explore the power of public commitments—why sharing your goals publicly can help you follow through—and how to use tracking systems to measure your progress and keep yourself honest.

Imagine having someone who celebrates your wins, helps you troubleshoot your struggles, and encourages you to keep going when motivation wanes. Picture yourself in a group of like-minded individuals, all rooting for each other's success. Accountability isn't just about external pressure—it's about building a community that supports you, strengthens you, and keeps you focused on the path ahead.

By the end of this chapter, you'll have the tools and strategies to build a system of accountability that works for you. You'll understand why going it alone often leads to inconsistency and how involving others in your journey can make all the difference. Let's explore how to transform your goals into shared commitments that inspire action, create consistency, and bring you closer to your vision.

8.1 ACCOUNTABILITY PARTNERS AND GROUPS

An accountability partner or group is one of the most powerful ways to stay on track with your goals. Sharing your progress with others makes you less likely to procrastinate or give up. Knowing that someone else is rooting for you—and checking in on you—creates a sense of responsibility that can be a game-changer for your commitment and follow-through.

Finding an Accountability Partner: An accountability partner understands your goals and is committed to helping you achieve them. This could be a friend, family member, colleague, or mentor. The key is finding someone reliable, supportive, and willing to be honest with you when you need it.

Benefits of an Accountability Partner

- **Support and Motivation:** Your partner will encourage you on difficult days and celebrate your wins with you.
- **Honest Feedback:** A good accountability partner will tell you the truth, even when it's hard to hear. They'll hold you accountable to your commitments.
- **Shared Progress:** Working alongside someone with similar goals can be inspiring as you witness each other's growth.

How to Choose the Right Partner

- **Look for Commitment:** Choose someone as committed to their own goals as you are to yours. Shared commitment creates a strong foundation.
- **Set Clear Expectations:** Agree on how often you'll check in (e.g., weekly, bi-weekly) and what format you'll use (phone calls, messages, or in-person meetings).
- **Be Open and Transparent:** An accountability partnership only works if you're honest. Be upfront about your progress, challenges, and what you need from your partner.

Example

If you are working on a fitness goal, an accountability partner could be someone who also wants to stay active. You could plan to work out together or check in daily to share updates. Knowing that someone expects you to report your progress makes it harder to skip a workout.

Joining an Accountability Group: While an individual partner is valuable, a group can provide even more support. Accountability groups bring together multiple people with similar goals, creating a community of encouragement, feedback, and shared motivation.

Types of Accountability Groups

- **Mastermind Groups**: These are small groups of people who meet regularly to discuss their goals, share advice, and provide support. Entrepreneurs, creatives, and professionals often use mastermind groups to advance in their fields.
- **Online Communities:** Countless online groups and forums focus on goals, from fitness to writing to financial independence. These groups provide a flexible way to connect, even if you don't meet in person.
- **Local Meetups:** If you prefer face-to-face interaction, local accountability groups or meetups can provide a supportive environment to share your progress and challenges.

Exercise

1. **Identify Potential Partners or Groups:** Think about people in your life who might make good accountability partners. Alternatively, search for online communities, local meetups, or mastermind groups related to your goals.
2. **Reach Out:** Once you've identified a potential partner or group, introduce yourself and share your goals. Don't be afraid to express what you hope to gain from the partnership.

3. **Set Up Regular Check-ins:** Schedule weekly, bi-weekly, or monthly check-ins and establish a format that works for both of you. Consistency in these meetings is crucial in keeping each other accountable.

8.2 MAKE YOUR GOALS VISIBLE

Making a public commitment is a powerful way to stay accountable. When you declare your goals to others, whether friends, family, or social media followers, you create a sense of external accountability. Public commitments are practical because they add social pressure; once you've announced your intentions, you feel a greater responsibility to follow through.

Why Public Commitments Work

Public commitments tap into the psychology of social accountability. Humans are naturally inclined to care about how others perceive them. When you tell people about your goals, you're essentially putting your reputation on the line. This external pressure makes you more likely to follow through.

Ways to Make Public Commitments

- **Announce Your Goal on social media:** Share your goal on platforms like Facebook, Instagram,

or LinkedIn. Posting updates regularly will keep your network informed of your progress and create a built-in audience that motivates you.
- **Tell Friends and Family:** Even if you don't want to make a social media announcement, telling close friends and family can be just as effective. Choose a few people who will support you and check your progress.
- **Participate in Public Challenges:** Join public challenges, like a 30-day fitness or a month-long writing challenge. These challenges are often community-based and come with set deadlines, making it harder to quit halfway through.

Example

If you're working on a goal to complete a half-marathon, consider posting about it on social media and updating your progress each week. The public announcement makes it harder to skip a training day, as you know others are following your journey.

Exercise

Choose a goal you're working on and decide how to make it public. Announce it on social media, tell a few supportive friends, or sign up for a public challenge. Commit to providing regular updates to keep yourself accountable and engaged.

8.3 STAY ACCOUNTABLE TO YOURSELF

While external accountability is valuable, holding yourself accountable is also essential. Tracking systems help you monitor your progress and keep your goals front and center. By consistently tracking your efforts, you create a visible record of your journey, reinforcing your commitment and making it harder to abandon your goals.

Types of Tracking Systems

- **Habit Trackers:** Habit trackers are simple but powerful tools for monitoring daily habits. You can use a habit-tracking app, a bullet journal, or a calendar where you mark off each day you complete a habit. Seeing your progress visually can be highly motivating.
- **Goal Tracking Apps:** Digital tools like Strides, Trello, and Notion allow you to set goals, create checklists, and review progress over time. These apps make it easy to stay organized and track multiple goals in one place.
- **Progress Journals:** Keeping a journal dedicated to your goals and progress can effectively hold you accountable. Use it to write down what you've achieved, any obstacles you faced, and how you plan to move forward. This habit of reflection builds self-awareness and motivation.

- **Weekly or Monthly Reviews:** Setting aside time each week or month to review your progress can be a powerful accountability tool. During these reviews, reflect on what went well, identify any challenges, and adjust your plan if needed. Regular reviews help you stay focused and prevent you from veering off course.

Example

If your goal is to save a certain amount of money by the end of the year, you could use a digital goal-tracking app to monitor your monthly savings progress. By setting up reminders and tracking your deposits, you'll be more aware of your progress and more likely to stay on target.

Exercise

Identify a tracking method that feels motivating and manageable for you. Whether it's an app, a physical habit tracker, or a weekly review journal, commit to using it consistently to monitor your progress. Tracking helps you stay accountable and gives you a clear view of how far you've come.

Why Accountability Matters

Accountability is essential for goal achievement because it helps transform your intentions into consistent actions. By sharing your progress with others, making public commitments, and using tracking systems, you create layers of accountability that keep you committed. Accountability keeps you honest, motivated, and focused, making it less likely that you'll abandon your goals when challenges arise.

You have someone in your corner, whether an accountability partner, a group, or a public audience, who provides support and encouragement. Tracking your progress reinforces your commitment by making each small step visible. Accountability isn't just a support system; it's a powerful tool for building momentum and making consistent progress.

Embracing Accountability for Success

Accountability is a game-changer for goal achievement. Whether it's a partner, a coach, or an online community, having someone in your corner makes all the difference. By creating accountability systems, making public commitments, and tracking your progress, you'll build momentum and stay committed to your goals. Accountability transforms intentions into actions, helping you stay on course.

In the next chapter, we'll discuss celebrating your wins. Every step forward, no matter how small, deserves recognition. Recognizing your progress reinforces your efforts and inspires you for the journey ahead.

* * * *

Action Steps

Reflect on the accountability strategies discussed in this chapter. Write down which approach feels most supportive for you—finding a partner, making a public commitment, or using a tracking system. Take one small action today to increase your accountability and commit to checking in regularly.

With accountability systems in place, it's time to celebrate your progress. In the next chapter, we'll explore the importance of recognizing your big and small wins to motivate and inspire you on your journey to success. Let's celebrate every step forward together.

Need help applying these strategies? Download the Vision to Victory Workbook and refer to Chapter 8 for more exercises, templates, and tools to guide you through every step.

9 CELEBRATE WINS

"The more you praise and celebrate your life, the more there is in life to celebrate." — Oprah Winfrey.

Imagine reaching a goal you've worked so hard to achieve—whether completing a challenging project, hitting a personal milestone, or finally forming a habit you've struggled with for months. What's the first thing you do? Do you pause to appreciate the effort and progress that got you there? Or do you rush past the accomplishment, already focusing on the next goal?

In our fast-paced, goal-oriented world, skipping the celebration and moving straight to the next task on the list is easy. But Oprah Winfrey's words remind us that celebration isn't just a luxury—it's a necessity. Every win, no matter how small, deserves recognition. Why? Because celebrating reinforces progress, builds confidence, and reminds us why we started the journey in the first place. Success is rarely achieved in one monumental leap; it results from countless small victories. Celebrating these moments doesn't just make the journey more enjoyable—it fuels your motivation to keep going.

Think about the last time you acknowledged your progress. Did you take pride in it or dismiss it as "not enough"? We often minimize our achievements because they don't feel significant enough compared to the "bigger" goals ahead. But each step forward is meaningful. No matter how small, each effort contributes to the momentum that will eventually carry you to your ultimate destination. Celebrating these wins isn't about indulging in empty praise—it's about validating the process, acknowledging your hard work, and encouraging yourself to keep pushing forward.

Research shows that celebrating progress activates the brain's reward system, releasing dopamine—the "feel-good" chemical associated with pleasure and motivation. This positive reinforcement makes you feel good in the moment and increases your likelihood of repeating the behavior that led to the success. In other words, celebrating small wins creates a feedback loop that keeps you on track and strengthens your commitment to your goals.

Celebrating isn't limited to the significant, once-in-a-lifetime milestones. It can—and should—be woven into your daily life. Whether completing a workout, hitting a savings goal, or even finishing a productive day at work, acknowledging these moments of progress keeps you connected to your journey. Celebrations can be as simple as a smile, a heartfelt "I did it," or a few moments of gratitude for how far you've come. They can also involve tangible rewards—a favorite meal, a fun outing, or treating yourself to something you've wanted. Whatever form it takes, celebrating reminds you that your efforts matter and that progress, no matter how small, is worth honoring.

This chapter will explore the transformative power of celebrating big and small wins. You'll learn why recognizing incremental progress is as important as achieving significant milestones. We'll dive into how creating reward systems can re-energize you, boost your motivation, and help you stay consistent on the path to success. Additionally, we'll discuss how tracking your progress and reflecting on your achievements can keep you connected to your goals and clarify the next steps.

By the end of this chapter, you'll have practical strategies to make celebration a consistent part of your journey. You'll understand how shifting your mindset to focus on progress rather than perfection can transform how you approach your goals. Let's take the time to honor every step forward, embrace the joy of the process, and cultivate a life filled with meaningful victories, one celebration at a time. Victories.

9.1 THE POWER OF SMALL WINS

When we think about success, we often focus on the end goal—the significant, life-changing accomplishment. But success is rarely the result of a single leap. It's built on small, consistent actions over time. Each small win brings you closer to your ultimate goal, and recognizing these victories helps you stay motivated on the journey.

Why Small Wins Matter

Psychologists have found that small wins create a positive feedback loop. Each small success triggers a dopamine release in the brain, which leads to feelings of pleasure and satisfaction. This boost in mood reinforces the behavior, making you more likely to continue working toward your goal. Celebrating small wins means actively training your brain to associate progress with positive emotions.

Celebrating small wins also helps combat the familiar feeling of overwhelm. Big goals can feel intimidating, especially if the path is long. But by focusing on small achievements along the way, you break down the journey into manageable steps, each deserving recognition. Small wins remind you that you're moving forward, even when the finish line is still far off.

Examples

Let's say your goal is to run a marathon. Some examples of small wins along the way might include:

- o   Completing your first 5K training run

- Hitting a new personal best for distance or speed
- Staying consistent with your training schedule for an entire month
- Recovering from a setback or injury and getting back on track

Each achievement, though small compared to the full marathon, is a meaningful step forward. Recognizing these wins motivates you and reminds you how far you've come.

Exercise

Think about a goal you're currently working toward. Make a list of small milestones or achievements that would mark progress. These could be daily, weekly, or monthly achievements. By identifying small wins in advance, you'll have a list of things to celebrate as you move forward.

9.2 REWARD SYSTEMS FOR MILESTONES

While celebrating small wins is important, setting up reward systems for more significant milestones along your journey is also helpful. A reward system gives you something to look forward to and incentivizes you to stay committed. By associating specific milestones with rewards, you reinforce that hard work and consistency lead to enjoyable outcomes.

Why Reward Systems Work

Reward systems are effective because they leverage the brain's natural reward circuitry. When we anticipate a reward, our brains release dopamine, which motivates us to take action. Rewards also create a sense of balance, reminding us that the journey is as valuable as the destination. Treating yourself along the way prevents burnout and keeps your energy levels high.

Types of Rewards

1. **Experiential Rewards:** These rewards involve doing something enjoyable, such as going out for a nice dinner, taking a weekend trip, or treating yourself to a spa day. Experiential rewards are memorable and can serve as a celebration of your hard work.
2. **Physical Rewards:** Physical rewards are tangible items, such as buying yourself a new book, clothing, or a gadget you've wanted. Physical rewards work well because they remind you of your achievement.
3. **Social Rewards:** Share your milestones with others and celebrate together. This could mean hosting a small gathering, posting about your progress on social media, or sharing your achievement with friends and family.
4. **Relaxation Rewards:** Sometimes, the best reward is simply permitting yourself to rest. For

example, after reaching a significant milestone, you might take a day off, sleep in, or enjoy a relaxing evening with no obligations.

Example

Imagine you're working on a goal to write a book. You might set up the following reward system:

- Milestone 1: Finish the outline – Treat yourself to your favorite dessert.
- Milestone 2: Complete the first three chapters – Buy yourself a new book or journal.
- Milestone 3: Reach the halfway point – Go for a nice dinner with friends.
- Milestone 4: Complete the first draft – Take a weekend getaway.
- Milestone 5: Finalize editing – Host a small celebration or dinner with friends and family.

This reward system gives you something to look forward to at each stage, keeping you motivated and adding enjoyment to the journey.

Exercise

Identify critical milestones for your current goal. For each milestone, choose a meaningful and motivating reward. Write down these rewards and keep them somewhere visible so you'll have a clear incentive to work toward each milestone.

9.3 TRACK SUCCESS AND REFLECTION

Celebrating wins and rewarding yourself is essential, but to sustain motivation, it's equally valuable to reflect on your progress. Regular reflection lets you see the bigger picture and recognize patterns in your efforts, helping you stay connected to your journey.

Why Tracking and Reflection Matter

Tracking your success provides a visual representation of your progress. When you see how far you've come, it boosts your confidence and reinforces your commitment. Conversely, reflection helps you gain insights into what's working, what's challenging, and how to adjust your approach if needed. Tracking and reflection are powerful tools for maintaining motivation and staying aligned with your goals.

Ways to Track Your Success

1. **Progress Journals:** Keep a journal where you document your achievements, big and small. Write down your daily, weekly, or monthly progress, noting any challenges you overcame and lessons you learned. A progress journal serves as a

personal record of your journey and can be inspiring to look back on.

2. **Milestone Charts:** Create a visual chart that tracks your progress toward major milestones. For example, if you're working on a fitness goal, you could create a chart that tracks each week of training or each pound lost. Visual charts make it easy to see how far you've come and keep you motivated.

3. **Digital Tools:** Apps like Strides, Trello, or Notion are great for tracking your progress on long-term goals. These tools allow you to set deadlines, check off completed tasks, and review your progress over time. Digital tracking tools are convenient and easy to update regularly.

Exercises

- **Weekly Review:** Set aside time to review your progress weekly. Ask yourself questions like: What did I accomplish this week? What challenges did I face? What am I proud of? This weekly reflection helps you recognize your efforts and reinforces your commitment.

- **Monthly Reflection:** At the end of each month, take a moment to look back at your progress. Write down any significant wins, lessons learned, or adjustments you want to make for the next month. Monthly reflections provide a broader view of your journey and help you focus on the bigger picture.

Example

Suppose you're working on a financial goal, such as saving a certain amount by the end of the year. You could set up a digital chart that tracks your monthly savings and, at the end of every month, reflects on your spending habits, challenges, and progress. This combination of tracking and reflection keeps you accountable and allows you to make adjustments as needed.

Exercise

Choose a method for tracking your progress, such as a journal, chart, or digital tool. Commit to a regular reflection schedule, such as a weekly or monthly review. Use this time to celebrate your wins, assess your progress, and make any adjustments needed to stay on track.

The Power of Celebrating Your Journey

Every small victory brings you closer to your ultimate goal. Celebrating your progress isn't just about having fun—it's crucial to staying motivated and connected to your journey. Recognizing your achievements, no matter how minor, reinforces the positive behaviors that lead to success. By celebrating each step forward, you build a mindset that values growth, resilience, and perseverance.

Remember, success is not just a destination; it's a journey filled with moments of growth and accomplishment. Each time you reach a milestone, take the time to celebrate and appreciate how far you've come. Celebrating doesn't just mark your progress; it fuels your journey, giving you the energy and motivation to keep moving forward.

The Joy of Celebrating Wins

Every step forward, no matter how small, is worth celebrating. Recognizing your progress keeps you motivated and reminds you that success is a journey, not just a destination. Celebrating wins, setting up meaningful rewards, and taking time for reflection create a positive feedback loop that makes your goals more enjoyable and fulfilling. Celebrating your wins builds resilience and gratitude, essential for sustained success.

In the next chapter, we'll explore how to stay committed to your vision and turn today's dreams into tomorrow's reality. With a clear purpose and a habit of celebrating progress, you'll be well-equipped to keep pushing forward.

* * * *

Action Steps

Write down a recent win you feel proud of, no matter how small. Please take a moment to reflect on what you learned and how it brought you closer to your goal. Commit to regularly celebrating your wins, and notice how it impacts your motivation and confidence.

With a practice of celebration in place, it's time to look ahead. In the next chapter, we'll dive into strategies for staying committed to your long-term vision, even when challenges arise. Let's continue on the path toward turning today's dreams into tomorrow's reality.

Need help applying these strategies? Download the Vision to Victory Workbook and refer to Chapter 9 for more exercises, templates, and tools to guide you through every step.

10 FROM VISION TO VICTORY

"The future belongs to those who believe in the beauty of their dreams." — Eleanor Roosevelt.

Dreams are among the most potent forces in life. They ignite our imagination, give us direction, and inspire us to overcome limitations. They give us something to work toward—a life filled with meaning, purpose, and fulfillment. Yet, as Eleanor Roosevelt reminds us, belief alone isn't enough to make our dreams a reality. The future isn't a gift that falls into our laps; it's something we must create. It takes courage to dream considerably and even more courage to back those dreams with focused action, perseverance, and the resilience to overcome challenges.

Think about where you started when you picked up this book. Maybe you had a vague idea of what you wanted but felt unsure of how to get there. Maybe you struggled with procrastination, lacked clarity, or doubted your ability to achieve your goals. Now, as you approach the end of this journey, take a moment to reflect on how far you've come. You've defined your "why," set meaningful goals, build habits that stick, created routines that empower you, and learned how to overcome obstacles like procrastination. Each chapter has added a new tool to your toolbox, preparing you to achieve your goals and pursue future ones confidently and clearly.

But here's the truth: achieving a goal is not the end—it's just one milestone in a lifelong process of growth and self-discovery. Success is not a destination; it's a journey, and the key to long-term fulfillment lies in your ability to keep growing, set new goals, and keep moving forward. Reaching one goal opens the door to new possibilities. Each success builds a foundation for even more remarkable achievements, and each challenge you overcome strengthens your ability to navigate the road ahead.

This chapter is about embracing that continual process. It's about recognizing that victory is not a single moment but a series of choices and actions over time. Reflecting on your progress allows you to appreciate how much you've accomplished while identifying areas for growth. Adjusting your goals ensures you remain aligned with your evolving vision and priorities. Sustaining success requires maintaining momentum, continually adapting to life's changes, staying open to new opportunities, and committing to lifelong learning.

The road from vision to victory doesn't end here. It's an ongoing cycle of dreaming, achieving, and growing. In this chapter, we'll take a step back to celebrate your progress and reflect on the lessons you've learned. We'll explore how to set new goals that challenge and inspire you while staying true to your vision. You'll learn strategies to maintain your momentum, such as practicing gratitude, staying adaptable in the face of change, and cultivating a mindset that embraces growth.

Imagine looking back on your life years from now, not regretfully but with pride—pride in the steps you took, the obstacles you overcame, and the life you built. Imagine a future where every goal you set brings you closer to becoming the person you want to be. That future is yours to shape. By reflecting on your journey, adjusting for the road ahead, and committing to sustained growth, you'll continue to move toward an even brighter, more fulfilling life.

Let's dive into the steps that will help you maintain your progress, build on your victories, and keep believing in the beauty of your dreams. The tools, habits, and routines you've developed are only the beginning. This is your moment to take everything you've learned and carry it forward into a future filled with limitless possibilities. The journey continues—and so does your growth.

10.1 REFLECT ON PROGRESS

Reflecting on your journey is essential for understanding how far you've come and recognizing your growth. Reflection isn't just about looking back; it's about drawing lessons from your experiences, celebrating your accomplishments, and identifying areas for improvement. By acknowledging your progress, you reinforce the habits and actions that have contributed to your success, strengthening your foundation for future goals.

Why Reflection Matters

Reflection allows you to see the bigger picture. Focusing on daily tasks and immediate goals makes it easy to lose sight of the broader journey. Reflecting on your progress helps you understand what has worked, what challenges you've overcome, and how your vision has evolved. It also provides a sense of accomplishment, crucial for maintaining motivation and confidence.

How to Reflect on Your Progress

1. **Review Milestones:** Review the milestones you set for yourself in earlier chapters. Which ones did you achieve? What small wins have you celebrated along the way? Reviewing these milestones helps you see the concrete steps you've taken toward your goals.

2. **Identify Key Lessons:** Consider any challenges or setbacks. What did you learn from these experiences? Reflecting on lessons learned helps you build resilience and prepares you for future obstacles.

3. **Celebrate Your Growth:** Recognize your external achievements and personal growth. Perhaps you've become more disciplined, resilient, or confident. Acknowledge these internal changes as part of your progress.

Exercise

Take a few moments to write down a reflection on your journey so far. Consider the milestones you've reached, the challenges you've overcome, and the personal growth you've experienced. This exercise will help you internalize your achievements and give you a sense of pride in how far you've come.

10.2 ADJUST FOR FUTURE GOALS

As you grow and evolve, your goals may shift, and that's a natural part of the journey. The goals that motivated you at the start of your journey may not be the same ones that inspire you now. Adjusting your goals doesn't mean abandoning your vision—it means adapting it to fit your current self, values, and aspirations.

Why Goal Adjustment is Necessary

Goal adjustment ensures that your goals align with your evolving vision and values. As you progress, you gain new insights and skills, and your perspective on what's possible may change. Regularly reassessing your goals ensures that you're moving in a direction that still resonates with you.

Steps for Adjusting Your Goals

1. **Revisit Your Vision Statement:** Review the vision statement you created in Chapter 3. Does it still resonate with you, or have you discovered new elements you want to incorporate? Your vision should be a living, evolving document that reflects your current dreams and ambitions.
2. **Set New Milestones:** Based on your reflections, set new milestones that align with your adjusted vision. These milestones could involve expanding on your previous goals, exploring new areas of interest, or pivoting in a different direction. Setting new milestones helps you create a roadmap for the next phase of your journey.
3. **Prioritize What Matters Most:** As you adjust your goals, focus on the most meaningful areas. Use the prioritization techniques from Chapter 7, like the Eisenhower Matrix, to ensure that your

energy is directed toward goals that align with your core values.

Example

Imagine you initially set a goal to advance in your career, aiming for a promotion within two years. However, through this journey, you have discovered a passion for entrepreneurship and decided that starting your business aligns better with your long-term vision. Adjusting your goals to reflect this new direction allows you to pursue what truly excites you rather than staying on a path that no longer fits.

Exercise

Spend some time revisiting your current goals. Ask yourself if they still reflect your vision and values. If they don't, adjust them to align with your current priorities. Write down any new milestones or steps you'd like to take moving forward.

10.3 MAINTAIN LONG-TERM SUCCESS

Reaching a significant goal is an accomplishment, but maintaining that success requires ongoing effort and commitment. Long-term success isn't about reaching a destination and stopping; it's about building habits, systems, and mindsets that keep you moving forward.

Focusing on sustainability ensures your progress supports your growth and happiness over time.

Why Long-Term Success Matters

Long-term success creates stability and a sense of fulfillment. Short-term achievements can bring satisfaction, but building a foundation for long-term growth ensures that your efforts lead to lasting change. Maintaining success involves continuously learning, adapting, and setting new goals that keep you challenged and engaged.

Strategies for Maintaining Long-Term Success

1. **Build Resilient Habits:** The habits you've developed on your journey are crucial in sustaining your success. Continue practicing the habits supporting your goals, and look for opportunities to refine and improve them. For example, if you developed a habit of daily exercise while working toward a fitness goal, maintaining that habit will help you stay healthy in the long run.
2. **Embrace Lifelong Learning:** Successful people don't stop learning once they've achieved a goal. Stay curious and open to new experiences. Take

courses, read books, attend workshops, and seek out mentors. Lifelong learning keeps you adaptable and helps you continue growing personally and professionally.

3. **Stay Connected to Your Why:** Your "why" drives your goals. Revisit the reasons that motivated you to start this journey in the first place. Staying connected to your "why" keeps you grounded and reminds you of the bigger purpose behind your efforts, making it easier to stay committed even when challenges arise.

4. **Reflect Regularly:** Just as you did in the reflection section, make reflection a regular part of your life. Set aside time each month, quarter, or year to review your goals, progress, and vision. Reflection allows you to celebrate your growth, recognize areas for improvement, and make necessary adjustments to your path.

Example

Your goal was to improve your financial health, and you successfully paid off debt over the last year. To maintain that success, you might set a new goal: build an emergency fund, create a long-term investment plan, and continue tracking your spending. By setting new financial goals, you ensure that your progress isn't temporary but part of a lasting journey toward financial security.

Exercise

Write down three habits or practices to help you maintain your progress. Consider how you can continue to grow in the areas that matter to you. These could include a commitment to ongoing learning, setting new goals, or revisiting your "why" regularly.

Victory as a Lifelong Journey

Victory isn't a single event—it results from consistent action over time. By setting clear goals, building supportive habits, and staying accountable, you've equipped yourself to overcome challenges and achieve your dreams. But remember, this is just the beginning. Success is a journey, not a destination, and with each step forward, you'll continue to grow, learn, and create the life you've always envisioned.

As you move forward, embrace the process and stay connected to your vision. Recognize that every achievement, every lesson, and every challenge is a part of your story. With each new goal, you'll expand your potential, refine your skills, and strengthen your resilience. This journey from vision to victory is a lifelong path of growth and fulfillment; you are ready to make it your own.

* * * *

Action Steps

Take a moment to reflect on your journey from vision to victory. Write down three lessons you've learned and three qualities you've developed. How has this journey shaped you, and what are you most proud of? Let this reflection remind you of your strength, commitment, and progress.

You have completed this journey through Vision to Victory, but your journey is far from over. Use the strategies you have learned in this book as tools to support your future goals, no matter how big or small.

Remember, every step you take brings you closer to your envisioned life. As you move forward, keep believing in the beauty of your dreams—and take action every day to make them a reality.

Need help applying these strategies? Download the Vision to Victory Workbook and refer to Chapter 10 for more exercises, templates, and tools to guide you through every step.

Conclusion

As you close this book, take a moment to reflect. Imagine looking back on the path you've traveled, the goals you've set, and the small steps you've taken to bring yourself closer to your dreams. See the moments of progress, the milestones you've achieved, and even the challenges you've overcome. Feel the strength and resilience you've built, and recognize how far you've come.

This journey from vision to victory is not just about reaching one destination—transforming your mindset, habits, and life. Every chapter, every exercise, and every strategy you have practiced is a building block that has brought you closer to the person you're becoming. You've not only learned how to set goals and build habits, but you've also developed the tools and confidence to turn any dream into reality. This is your victory—not just in the result but in each step of growth and commitment.

Summary

In this book, we started by helping you define your vision—a powerful image of the life you want to create. From there, you identify your "why," the deep-rooted purpose that fuels your dreams. With that foundation, you learned to set SMART goals, craft a personal vision statement, and design a clear, actionable path forward.

You discovered the importance of building habits, creating routines, and prioritizing tasks to keep you moving consistently toward your goals.

Along the way, you tackled one of the biggest obstacles to progress: procrastination. You learned strategies to overcome hesitation, break tasks into manageable steps, and take action, even when motivation was low. You also developed systems for planning, prioritizing, and holding yourself accountable, ensuring your focus remained on what truly matters. You built a support system through accountability partnerships, public commitments, and tracking systems, creating a framework that reinforces your commitment and inspires you.

Finally, you recognized the importance of celebrating your wins. Each small victory, milestone achieved, and step forward became an opportunity to honor your progress and boost your motivation. As you reached the final chapters, you reflected on your journey, adjusted your goals, and committed to maintaining long-term success. By the end, you realize that victory isn't a single destination but a lifelong journey of growth, learning, and fulfillment.

This journey from vision to victory has equipped you with practical tools, proven strategies, and a new mindset. You have everything you need to turn your biggest dreams into reality, one step at a time.

Revisit and Apply

As you move forward, remember that growth and progress are ongoing processes. The strategies you have learned are not meant to be used just once—they're tools to support you throughout your life. Revisit them often, especially during uncertainty, challenge, or change. Each time you return to these strategies, you'll find new insights, more profound clarity, and renewed motivation.

Whether setting new goals, adjusting your vision, or facing unexpected obstacles, these strategies will continue to serve you. Building a life of purpose and fulfillment isn't about perfection or speed; it's about consistency, resilience, and a willingness to keep going, even when the path isn't easy. Embrace each step as part of the journey, and remember that every small action, no matter how insignificant it may seem, brings you closer to your vision.

Consider this book a guide that you can return to again and again. When you're feeling stuck, review the chapters on overcoming procrastination. When you need direction, revisit the sections on planning and prioritizing. When celebrating a significant milestone, read the chapter on recognizing your wins and allow yourself to appreciate your progress. Each chapter and each strategy is a resource to help you stay aligned with your vision and keep moving forward.

FINAL BOOST

As you take the first step beyond this book, remember: "The first step may seem small, but every great achievement begins with a single step." Greatness doesn't happen overnight. Success is not the result of one grand action but countless small steps taken with purpose and intention. Trust in the power of those small steps. Trust your ability to overcome challenges, adapt, grow, and achieve your dreams.

You have everything you need within you to make your vision a reality. The journey from vision to victory is one of courage, resilience, and faith in yourself. Keep believing in the beauty of your dreams, and keep taking steps—no matter how small or uncertain. Each step forward brings you closer to the life you've always envisioned.

Your journey doesn't end here. This is just the beginning. Every day, you can create a life that aligns with your values, fulfills your passions, and reflects your best version of yourself. So take that first step, the next, and then the next. Embrace the journey, celebrate the victories, and keep moving forward. Your vision awaits, and you're turning it into your victory with each step.

A Personal Challenge

As you close this book, I challenge you to act on something you have been dreaming about immediately. Choose one small, actionable step you can take today that aligns with your vision and brings you closer to your goals. It doesn't have to be significant. It could be as simple as writing down your goals, reaching out to a potential accountability partner, or setting a date for your next milestone.

Commit to taking this one step, and let it be the beginning of your journey from vision to victory. Please take a deep breath, trust in the process, and remember: the future belongs to those who believe in the beauty of their dreams and are willing to take action to make them a reality.

* * * *

YOUR NEXT STEP TO SUCCESS

Download Your Free Vision to Victory Workbook

Congratulations on completing Vision to Victory!

You have gained powerful insights into goal-setting, habit-building, and achieving your dreams. Now, it's time to turn what you've learned into action. To help you do that, I have created the Vision to Victory Workbook, a free companion resource designed to guide you every step of the way.

Scan the QR Code or click the image below to download the free workbook. Then, please enter your email to receive it instantly!

"The difference between a dream and a goal is action. Start your journey today."

APPENDICES

The following resources are designed to support you as you apply the principles and strategies from Vision to Victory. Use these templates and tools as guides to help you set goals, track habits, create effective routines, and continue learning and growing. Each appendix is a practical step toward turning your dreams into reality.

APPENDIX A: SMART GOAL PLANNER TEMPLATE

Setting SMART (Specific, Measurable, Achievable, Relevant, and Time-bound) goals is one of the foundational strategies discussed in this book. The SMART Goal Planner Template helps you break down each component of your goal, creating a clear and actionable plan for success. Use this template when setting a new goal or revisiting an existing one.

SMART Goal Planner Template

SMART Component	Guiding Questions	Your Responses
Specific	What exactly do you want to achieve? Describe your goal in detail.	
Measurable	How will you measure progress? What indicators will tell you that you're on track?	
Achievable	Is this goal realistic? What	

	resources (time, skills, support) do you need?	
Relevant	Why is this goal important to you? How does it align with your vision and values?	
Time-bound	| What is your target deadline? Are there any milestones you can set along the way?	

Instructions for Using the Template

- **Define Your Goal:** Write your goal in the "Specific" row. Be as clear and detailed as possible.
- **Determine Metrics:** In the "Measurable" row, identify how you will measure your progress. This could be numbers, milestones, or specific outcomes.
- **Evaluate Feasibility:** In the "Achievable" row, assess whether the goal is realistic. List any resources or support you'll need to succeed.
- **Align with Your Values:** In the "Relevant" row, explain why this goal matters to you. This ensures you're motivated and connected to the outcome.
- **Set a Timeline:** In the "Time-bound" row, set a deadline and any smaller milestones to help you stay on track.

By following these steps, you'll create a SMART goal that is clear, actionable, and aligned with your vision.

APPENDIX B: HABIT TRACKER SHEET

Building and maintaining habits is essential for long-term success. The Habit Tracker Sheet provides a simple way to monitor your daily habits and see your progress over time. This tool is ideal for tracking any habit, from exercising to reading to practicing a skill. Habit tracking reinforces consistency and helps you stay accountable.

Habit Tracker Sheet Template

Habit	Day 1	Day 2	Day 3	Day 4	Day 5	Day 6	Day 7
Habit 1							
Habit 2							
Habit 3							

Instructions for Using the Habit Tracker Sheet

- **Identify Your Habits:** Write down the habits you want to track at the start of each week or month in the left column.
- **Track Daily Progress:** Mark off whether you completed the habit each day. You can use checkmarks, symbols, or colors to represent your progress.

- **Reflect at the End of the Week:** Review your progress. Are there any patterns? Which habits were consistent, and which need more attention?
- **Adjust as Needed:** Based on your reflection, make any adjustments to your habits or approach.

Using a habit tracker allows you to see your consistency visually, which reinforces the behavior and helps you build lasting habits.

APPENDIX C: DAILY ROUTINE CHECKLIST

An effective daily routine helps you start and end each day with purpose. The Daily Routine Checklist organizes your morning and evening routines, making it easier to stay consistent and focused on your goals. Use this checklist to create routines that support your productivity, health, and personal growth.

Daily Routine Checklist Template

Time of Day	Routine Item	Completed? (✓)
Morning Routine	Wake up at a consistent time.	
	Practice mindfulness or gratitude.	
	Exercise or stretch	
	Review goals or set intentions.	
	Eat a healthy breakfast.	

	Evening Routine	Reflect on the day's achievements.	
		Plan or prioritize tasks for tomorrow.	
		Unplug and disconnect from screens.	
		Practice relaxation techniques	
		Go to bed at a consistent time.	

Instructions for Using the Daily Routine Checklist:

- **Customize Your Routines**: Use the checklist above as a starting point, but feel free to customize it to fit your personal goals and lifestyle.
- **Check Off Each Task:** As you go through your day, mark off each completed item. This will help you stay accountable to your routine.
- **Reflect on Your Routine:** Review your routine at the end of the week. Are there tasks you struggled to complete? Are there adjustments you'd like to make?
- **Revise as Needed**: As your goals evolve, update your checklist to align it with your current priorities.

Following a consistent daily routine helps create momentum, reduces decision fatigue, and builds positive habits that move you closer to your goals.

APPENDIX D: RECOMMENDED BOOKS AND RESOURCES

The journey to achieving your dreams and mastering your goals is ongoing, and there is always more to learn. Below is a list of recommended books and resources to deepen your understanding of goal-setting, personal growth, productivity, and habit formation. These resources provide insights and inspiration from some of the most influential voices in personal development.

Books on Goal-Setting and Achievement

- **"Atomic Habits" by James Clear**: This book explores the science of habit formation and provides actionable strategies for building good habits and breaking bad ones. Clear's insights into the power of tiny changes are invaluable for anyone committed to long-term success.
- **"The 7 Habits of Highly Effective People" by Stephen R. Covey:** Covey's classic book outlines essential habits that lead to personal and professional effectiveness. His productivity and

goal-setting approach emphasizes proactivity, prioritization, and long-term vision.

- **"Grit: The Power of Passion and Perseverance" by Angela Duckworth:** Duckworth's research focuses on the role of grit—passion and perseverance—in achieving long-term goals. Her findings underscore the importance of resilience and staying committed to one's vision.

Books on Productivity and Time Management

- **"Deep Work: Rules for Focused Success in a Distracted World" by Cal Newport:** This book offers strategies for achieving high levels of focus and productivity by eliminating distractions. Newport's insights are handy for those who struggle to concentrate on their goals.
- **"Getting Things Done: The Art of Stress-Free Productivity" by David Allen:** Allen's book introduces a systematic approach to organizing tasks and responsibilities. His "GTD" method is widely recognized for its effectiveness in managing complex projects and maintaining focus.

Books on Personal Growth and Mindset

- **"Mindset: The New Psychology of Success" by Carol S. Dweck:** Dweck's research on growth mindset explains why believing in your ability to grow and improve is essential for success. This book is foundational for developing a resilient and open-minded approach to challenges.
- **"The Power of Now" by Eckhart Tolle:** This spiritual classic encourages readers to focus on the present moment. Tolle's insights can help reduce stress and create a sense of peace, allowing for a more balanced approach to achieving goals.

Additional Resources

- **TED Talks:** Many TED Talks by thought leaders in productivity, psychology, and personal growth offer quick and accessible insights into goal achievement and habit formation.
- **Online Courses:** Platforms like Coursera, Udemy, and LinkedIn Learning provide courses on goal-setting, productivity, and personal development taught by experts in the field.
- **Podcasts:** The Tim Ferriss Show, The Tony Robbins Podcast, and The School of Greatness feature interviews with successful people across industries who share their stories, habits, and tips for achieving greatness.

How to Use These Resources:

- **Start with One Book:** Choose one book from the list that aligns with your current needs and interests. Focus on applying its principles before moving on to the next.
- **Explore Online Courses or Podcasts:** Incorporate learning into your daily routine by listening to a podcast episode during your commute or dedicating time each week to an online course.
- **Reflect and Apply:** As you read, listen, or watch, take notes and consider how the insights relate to your goals. Make a habit of integrating these lessons into your life.

These appendices provide practical tools and resources to support your journey from vision to victory. Remember, the templates are just starting points—customize them to fit your unique goals and lifestyle. And keep learning, keep growing, and keep pushing forward. Your journey to success is ongoing, and with these resources, you can keep moving closer to the life you envision.

Acknowledgments

Writing Vision to Victory has been an incredible journey, and I'm deeply grateful to everyone who supported me along the way.

Thank you to my mentors and teachers for shaping my understanding of growth and goal-setting. To my family, especially my parents and spouse—your unwavering support and belief in me have been my greatest strength.

To my friends—thank you for your feedback and encouragement throughout this process.

Finally, to you, the reader—this book was written to empower you to pursue your dreams. Thank you for allowing me to be part of your journey.

With gratitude,

Dilip Patil

NEXT IN THE GOAL MASTERY SERIES

"Success isn't achieved in a single leap. It's built step-by-step, daily, through small actions that compound over time."

Congratulations on completing Vision to Victory! You've learned to set clear goals, build empowering habits, and take focused action to bring your dreams to life. But the journey doesn't end here.

In my upcoming book, The Power of Daily Progress, we'll dive into the secret to sustained success: the art of small, consistent actions. You'll discover how even two minutes daily can spark lasting change, overcome inertia, and create unstoppable momentum. This next book will show you how to harness the power of "small wins" to build confidence, maintain motivation, and stay resilient on your journey.

What You'll Learn in The Power of Daily Progress

- How to Break Down Big Goals into manageable daily actions so you always know exactly what to do next.
- Techniques for Staying Consistent even on low motivation days, ensuring you never lose sight of your vision.

- The Science of Small Wins and how celebrating daily progress builds confidence and keeps you on track.

Prepare to take your goal mastery skills to the next level and transform progress into a daily habit. The Power of Daily Progress is your guide to building the momentum you need to achieve extraordinary results, one small step at a time.

Stay tuned for the next step in your journey to success!

SHARE YOUR EXPERIENCE

Thank you for reading Vision to Victory! I hope this book has given you practical tools and fresh inspiration to pursue your goals with clarity and purpose. As a self-published author, your feedback is invaluable—it helps other readers find this book and guides me in creating more resources to support you.

If Vision to Victory made a difference in your journey, I would be grateful if you could take a moment to share your thoughts. Here are a few questions to consider as you reflect on your experience:

1. What was the most helpful idea or strategy in this book?
2. Did any chapter or exercise particularly resonate with you?
3. How has Vision to Victory impacted your approach to setting and achieving goals?
4. Would you recommend this book to others pursuing similar goals?
5. Is there anything you'd like to see in future books in the Goal Mastery Series?

Your review makes a real difference, especially on platforms like Amazon, Goodreads, or even social media, where other readers can discover this book. Search for

Vision to Victory by Dilip Patil on these platforms and click "Write a Review." Or you can write to me at patildilip23@gmail.com

Thank you for being a part of this journey and supporting independent authors like me. Your insights and feedback inspire me to keep writing and creating.

With gratitude,

Dilip Patil

ABOUT THE AUTHOR

Dilip Patil is a seasoned author, speaker, and mentor passionate about helping individuals achieve their fullest potential. With an established body of work in personal growth, goal-setting, and productivity, Dilip has dedicated his career to empowering readers with practical strategies for achieving success and living a purposeful life.

As the author of several acclaimed books, Dilip brings a wealth of experience and insight to his writing. His approach to personal development is grounded in real-world experience, combining proven techniques with a deep understanding of the human drive for growth and fulfillment. Through his books, Dilip has inspired thousands of individuals to take control of their lives, overcome obstacles, and pursue their dreams with clarity and commitment.

A Trusted Guide on the Journey to Success

Dilip's journey into personal development was driven by a desire to understand what truly fuels achievement and happiness. After years of research, personal experiences, and working with individuals from various backgrounds, he discovered the transformative power of clear goals, disciplined habits, and a resilient mindset. This understanding led to the creation of the Goal Mastery Series, a comprehensive collection of guides that walk readers through every step of their journey from vision to victory.

Vision to Victory is the latest addition to the Goal Mastery Series and builds on the principles introduced in Dilip's previous books. Focusing on defining meaningful goals, building effective habits, and maintaining motivation, this book is a practical roadmap for anyone ready to turn their aspirations into reality. Dilip's approachable style and actionable insights have made his work a trusted resource for readers seeking lasting change.

Stay Connected with Dilip Patil

Dilip values connection and community, and he welcomes readers to join him as they continue their journey toward personal and professional growth. Whether you're new to his work or have been following his books for years, Dilip is dedicated to providing ongoing support, insights, and inspiration.

https://www.facebook.com/dilip.patil.3979

https://www.linkedin.com/in/dilip-patil-4066a518

https://www.instagram.com/dilip.patil.3979

https://patildilip23.medium.com

Dilip Patil is committed to helping you achieve your biggest dreams, one step at a time. His books reflect his mission: to guide you on personal mastery so that each day brings you closer to the life you envision.

Connect with Dilip today and join a community dedicated to growth, resilience, and the pursuit of victory.

OTHER BOOKS BY DILIP PATIL

Vision to Victory is just one part of a comprehensive journey toward personal growth and goal achievement. Dilip Patil's other works dive deeper into various aspects of self-mastery, resilience, and the pursuit of success. Each book is designed to guide you through different phases of your personal and professional journey, providing practical tools, motivational insights, and actionable strategies to help you reach your fullest potential. Explore the following titles by Dilip Patil and continue building the life you envision:

Through his other esteemed book series, **"THE ART OF SUCCESS," "PROCRASTINATION TRIUMPH," and "LEADERSHIP TRANSFORMED,"** he delves into varied personal and professional growth facets. Each series offers a unique perspective on mastering life's challenges and seizing opportunities for success.

HAPPINESS JOURNEY

1. Daily Joy: Discover Contentment, Peace, Purpose, and Growth for a Happiness Journey.
2. True Bliss: Achieve Positivity, Balance, Fulfillment, and Harmony for a Happiness Journey.

3. Inner Peace: Cultivate Calm, Strength, Clarity, and Joy for a Lasting Happiness Journey"
4. LIFE'S JOY: Embrace Gratitude, Resilience, Simplicity, and Clarity for a Happiness Journey
5. Endless Serenity: Unlock Tranquility, Empowerment, Vitality, and Well-being for a Profound Happiness Journey

PROCRASTINATION TRIUMPH SERIES

1. Achieve It Now: Beat Procrastination for a Brighter Tomorrow is essential to overcoming procrastination and improving the future.
2. Temporal Triumph: Defeat Procrastination, Embrace Time Mastery, and Achieve Your Destiny.
3. Action Accelerator: Practical Strategies to Eliminate Procrastination, Propel Your Life and Career Forward.
4. Pathway Pioneer: Overcome Procrastination Through Strategic Habit and Build for Lasting Growth.
5. Success Sculptor: Crafting Habits, Conquering Procrastination, Achieving Goals, and Creating a Path to Enduring Success.

THE ART OF SUCCESS SERIES

1. Empowering Yourself to Achieve Success: This title empowers you to cultivate a mindset conducive to success and fulfillment. It guides you on a transformative exploration of personal development guided by core principles, actionable strategies, and inspiring anecdotes.
2. The Path to Lasting Happiness: Discover the keys to enduring happiness, navigating aspects like purpose, mindset, relationships, resilience, and more. Develop communication finesse, nurture empathy, and acquire skills for multifaceted success.
3. Yoga Flow for Tech Minds: This title harmonizes ancient wisdom with modern science to enhance productivity, reduce stress, and foster holistic well-being in the digital age. It offers practices tailored for tech minds seeking balance.
4. The Success Habits: Delve into the psychology of success to instill winning habits and unlock your full potential. Equip yourself with actionable strategies to elevate your productivity, career, and overall fulfillment.
5. The Success Mindset: Discover the secrets to attaining goals and crafting your desired reality. Learn how to nurture a winning mindset,

dismantle limiting beliefs, and unleash boundless potential.

6. Endurance: Journey deep into enduring and transcending life's tests—an invaluable companion on your path of growth and adaptability.

7. The Power of Adaptability: This book complements The Success Formula by exploring adaptability's remarkable influence on shaping destinies.

8. The Success Formula: Unlock success and potential with fundamental principles, tools, and real-life stories. This guide acts as a compass for personal and professional excellence.

9. Discover the Power of Gratitude: Explore the transformative power of gratitude in personal and professional growth.

10. 10 Pillars of Personal Growth: Embrace resilience, Foster Connections, Cultivate Well-being, and Reach the Zenith of Success.

LEADERSHIP TRANSFORMED

1. Leadership Awakening: Ignite Self-Awareness, Build Confidence, Foster Growth, And Embark on Your Leadership Journey

2. Visionary Pathways: Unleash Creativity, Foster Resilience, Amplify Impact, and Master Transformational Leadership

3. Masterful Communication: Enhance Influence, Improve Relationships, Boost Persuasion and Transform Leadership Skills
4. Decision Dynamics: Navigate Complexity, Solve Problems, Cultivate Impact, and Empower Leadership through Strategy
5. Empathy & Empowerment: Connect Deeply, Empower Others, Build Trust, and Create Resonant Leadership
6. Innovative Edge: Foster Creativity, Lead Change, Embrace Challenges, and Shape Modern Leadership
7. Resilient Resolve: Overcome Adversity, Maintain Focus, Cultivate Grit, and Build Unstoppable Leadership
8. Legacy Creation: Influence Generations, Achieve Goals, Transform Lives, and Elevate Your Leadership Impact

Each book in the series builds on the last, providing a complete arsenal for personal and professional success. To explore these titles further and for purchasing information, please visit https://www.amazon.com/author/patildilip.